TEACHING CHIPMUNKS TO
DANCE

TEACHING CHIPMUNKS TO
DANCE

THE BUSINESS LEADERS' GUIDE TO MAKING THE DISTRIBUTED ENTERPRISE YEAR 2000 COMPLIANT

BY
CHRIS JESSE

KENDALL/HUNT PUBLISHING COMPANY
4050 Westmark Drive   Dubuque, Iowa   52002
(800) 228-0810

Published by
Kendall/Hunt Publishing Company
Dubuque, Iowa
(800) 228-0810

Cover and text illustration: Kathrine Forster Kuo
Copy Editor: Bonnie Tilson

Library of Congress Catalog Card Number: 97-75584

ISBN 0-7872-4613-1

Printed in the United States of America

10 9 8 7 6 5 4 3 2

For you Judi. Home is looking in your eyes; contentment is hearing your laughter.

TIME, MANKIND, AND COMPLIANCE

These two things...past and future are but a single tide that unknowingly glides us across the present to a shore of repeated tragedy. This is the sum of it: you either go along or turn and face the current, chancing that desperate swim that leads away from yesterday. And if you do, you shall struggle and struggle and struggle, but there is no other way...for you either drift helplessly into fate or thrash valiantly toward a better tomorrow.

• CONTENTS •

CONTENTS

PREFACE
(FROM AN ANONYMOUS BENEFACTOR)

...and to the readers (those responsible for Year 2000 enterprise compliance) I bequeath my zoo, complete with all the animals, facilities, budget constraints, and various food stuffs. I bequeath my zoo in total, with the following admonishment: The rhinoceros needs to be inoculated, the pig smells funny, the elephant will not come out from underneath his blanket, and I can't explain it, but there are chipmunks all over the place. Oh yes, you had better make sure these critters don't hurt anybody. There's not enough liability insurance in the world to cover the kind of damage these rascals can inflict.

Confused? Let me do a little translation. The animals represent the distributed enterprise—a conglomeration of enterprise applications and desktops that are not Year 2000 compliant. The facilities are the various departments, job titles, platforms, and business functions that are infected with these noncompliant applications. Budget constraints depict the funding problems encountered in trying to make the enterprise compliant. Finally, the food stuffs portray the sustenance of the compliance effort (i.e., the fixes).

This zoo of Year 2000 issues has the capacity to do irreparable harm to those who ignore them. They are a time bomb that was activated decades ago by well-meaning programmers who developed very functional code with but a single flaw—they represented the year as a two-digit field. A small error indeed, but one with immense consequences.

And what about the chipmunks, rhinoceros, pig, and elephant? We are going to spend more time with them (and their friends) as we encounter and discuss the challenges and methods of making the distributed enterprise Year 2000 compliant. Enterprise Year 2000 compliance—some have called it impossible; others have labeled it a fool's errand. But as we shall see, it is neither foolish nor impossible. It is simply a matter of teaching chipmunks to dance.

ACKNOWLEDGMENTS

Those of you who know me understand that writing a book does not come easily to me. I am a man of limited abilities, and if this book speaks to you, it does so through the contributions of others. Accordingly, I would first like to thank God for bringing all these contributors into my life. You will see their names below, but I will never be able to fully explain how important these people are to me as contributors, friends, and family.

For those who saw possibilities in this topic and forced this book upon me, I offer my admiration and thanks. Teresa Poppen and Allison Legge, this book is bound with your sacrifice, will, and vision.

To the editors, all I can say is that I am sorry you had to work so hard. Your efforts are both known and appreciated. Thank you Tracey Minnich, Jae Cody, Jeanann Agiovlassitis, Lori Schwind Murray, and Nancy Dunn.

Ideas abound, but great ideas are precious. I have been blessed with many contributors who have brought vast experience and wisdom to this text. Thank you Steve Kuekes, Steve Groetzinger, Ted Kennedy, Jim Reece, Kevin Coggins, Tres Prince, Chuck Root of Safeguard Scientifics, Inc., Joe Pucciarelli of Gartner Group, Chris Germann of Gartner Group, Carl Wilson of Marriott International, Inc., and the scores of information technology professionals who are too numerous to mention individually.

Those involved in the production of the book deserve no less credit. Kathrine Kuo (the cover and artwork designer), Bonnie Tilson (the outside editor), Bob Englander (the indexer), and of course the staff at the publisher, Kendall/Hunt Publishing Company—each of you made a tremendous contribution. Thank you ladies and gentlemen.

Finally, I would like to thank my family. These are the folks who had to live with me during the many nights and weekends that this book has consumed. They, too, are the source of many of the anecdotes contained in the text. Thank you my children (in birth order), Rob, Mary, Rachel, and Amanda. You guys have been my greatest teachers. I thank my mother, Kay, for looking after the home front while I was away writing. And my most sincere thanks to my wife, Judi, who punctuated this effort with frequent laughter.

Oh yes, lest any of us become too focused on our contribution, I would like to offer my greatest thanks to Laverne (my dog). You were always there with a cold nose and an encouraging wimp. Thanks Laverne. Yes, I will give you another cookie.

There you have it, those who brought value to this book. As for those parts of the book that are lacking, they are mine. I can only apologize and assure the reader that it was my best effort.

INTRODUCTION

This book is the result of a long series of miscalculations and unexpected consequences. In fact, it was never supposed to be a book. It started out as a new chapter for the third edition of my previously published work, *A Journey Through Oz: The Business Leaders' Road Map to Tracking Information Technology Assets*, which addresses the subject of enterprise asset tracking. *Oz* was written to explain the advantage and methodology of proactively managing the distributed enterprise of clients and servers. As the number of available copies of *Oz* dwindled, those individuals who run my life insisted that the third edition had to address the topic of Year 2000 compliance for the distributed enterprise. I, having given scores of talks on the topic, flippantly agreed to write the chapter. This was my first mistake.

Having procrastinated the task until it approached the publisher's deadline, I took my notebook computer with me on vacation, promising to return with a draft of the required chapter. My wife, Judi, upon hearing that I might do some writing on the Year 2000 while at the beach, immediately expressed her reservations with the comment, "Oh no, another book!" No, no, I explained, just a chapter, just a chapter. "I don't think so; I don't think so," she said. "Too much experience and too much paper; want to place a little wager?" she asked. And so we come to mistake number two, my $100 bet with Judi that I would just write a chapter.

Toward the end of my vacation, I noticed I was on page 50, and there was no end in sight. I don't want to say that Judi razzed me about this; but if her sarcastic remarks were pinpricks, you could use me to strain clear liquids. I still had hope, however, as I fully expected those initially requesting a chapter to demand that I condense the material into fewer than twenty pages. This hope was short-lived, however, as the gatekeeper on such matters, Teresa, my friend and colleague, completed her review with an enthusiastic, "Keep going. There's a real need for material on this topic."

As the weeks passed and the book effort began to blur over a long series of nights and weekends, I began to see a pattern to what I had written. Clearly, there was an animal theme to my allegories. I did not worry about this folly, for I was certain that someone would scream at the thought of animals romping through a book on technology. Once again, I showed the foresight of a turnip, for not only did the editors like the animals, they wanted me to work one into the title.

So here it is, a 123-page chapter on Year 2000 enterprise compliance, sprinkled with animals and released in book form. I have elected to write this text in a slightly humorous tone, but the topic is a sober one. Both companies and careers will be ruined as a result of not fully understanding the impact of Year 2000 compliance on the distributed enterprise. We will see countless lawsuits lost as hundreds of defendants testify, "We didn't know that…we didn't understand that…there was no way of determining the extent that…desktops were computing bad dates and producing erroneous results."

There is, however, a way to know, understand, and quantify the compliance problems facing the distributed enterprise. Further, there is a means of correcting these problems before they do harm. That is what this book is about. I hope it occasionally makes you smile; but more importantly, I hope it helps to prepare you and your organization for the coming century.

TEACHING CHIPMUNKS TO
DANCE

CHAPTER 1

• BLANKETED ELEPHANTS •
THE PROBLEM DEFINED

Me: (*10:30 P.M. at the Springfield airport after a flight from Chicago*) Could you take me to the Ramada Inn next to the hospital, please?

Taxi Driver: In Springfield?

Me: Yes.

Taxi Driver: Sorry buddy, but I've been hacking in Springfield twenty-five years and there ain't no such place.

Me: I have it right here on my itinerary, 147 Trail Street.

Taxi Driver: Sorry, don't know Trail Street either.

Me: (*Irritated*) Wait here. I have a phone number. I'll call for directions.

Phone Operator: I'm sorry sir, but that is not a valid exchange. What area code are you calling?

Me: Two one seven.

Phone Operator: Sir, that is an Illinois area code. Do you want me to connect you to a long-distance operator?

Me: What state is this?

Operator: Missouri.

Me: Never mind.

Anyone who has traveled extensively has experienced a "near miss" in getting on the wrong plane. Unfortunately, I skipped the "near" part and actually boarded a plane that took me to Springfield, Missouri, instead of Springfield, Illinois. After several hours of driving (to Springfield, Illinois), my boss and I ended up having to share the last available room at the Pioneer Motor Lodge.

This would seem to be a good place to end this story, except for the suspect nature of our quarters that night. Our room was hard to describe; it was actually more of a conference room than a bedroom. As you entered, the first things you noticed were eighty folding chairs arranged in ten rows. Behind the chairs were two folding screens, and behind those, a pair of twin beds and the door to the bathroom. This, of course, seemed odd to us, but most things seem odd at 2:30 in the morning. So we set the alarm for 7:30 A.M. and went to sleep.

As it turned out, we would not need the alarm, for at 6:30 A.M. we found ourselves standing next to our beds at attention, in our underwear, hearts pounding, as we listened to a man with the advantage of a very capable audio system announce the opening and closing prices for hog bellies. I (still in my underwear) peered around the edge of the screen and discovered several things: first, there were eighty farmers gathered in our hotel room for their weekly Pork Producers Meeting; second, exiting the room required me to walk down the center aisle and turn left directly in front of the podium in order to reach the door; and third, certain elephants can indeed hide under blankets.

The hidden elephant I faced back in 1975 was that I had landed in the wrong state and was sleeping in what was obviously a conference room. The hidden elephant we address today is managing the Year 2000 across the distributed enterprise. Ironically, these two different elephants both successfully hid under a common blanket—our tendency to miss the panorama of our situation while we address the immediate issues at hand. For you see, I caught the flight and found a room, just as most of us have a plan to fix our errant Year 2000 programs (code). Unfortunately, I landed in the wrong state and attended a meeting in my underwear. Just as today we almost exclusively direct our Year 2000 compliance efforts toward central facilities, while ignoring the behemoth of desktops and servers collectively known as the distributed enterprise.

There is no doubt about it. The Year 2000 problem, as it applies to the distributed enterprise, is one very large and very ugly elephant. Before discussing the care and feeding of this beast, however, it is prudent to review the basics of the problem, specifically how the distributed enterprise is affected.

SOME OLD NEW MATH

We begin this discussion with some strange mathematics. The basics of the Year 2000 problem are as simple as understanding that 00 - 48 = 52. For those of us who grew up in the computer industry during the sixties and seventies, there is a logic to this convoluted equation. Most of us, however, are stuck with Mrs. Moore's (my fourth-grade teacher) reasoning that 0 - 48 = -48. To understand how both answers can be "correct" is to understand the essence of the Year 2000 quagmire.

The above mystery math was born in the sixties when computing power was hundreds of times more expensive than it is today. The great cost of computing services caused those using them to creatively conserve these valuable resources. One such bit of ingenuity involved a particularly scarce resource called computer memory. Of equal concern in those days was the optimum use of storage (disk space). Making the most of these two scarce commodities led to some creative programming, and ultimately to our problem.

To the best of my knowledge, no one knows who came up with the trick that led to the Year 2000 problem, but I suspect his name was

Waldo. I imagine Waldo working late into the night, studying a stack of computer printouts that listed column after column of dates. It was during this review that he noticed that each date had eight digits: two for the day, two for the month, and four for the year. But then his great discovery—every year on every date listed started with 19—1964, 1945, 1968, etc. "Why," Waldo mused, "should we waste valuable memory and storage on something that is always the same? Why not just calculate and store dates with the year abbreviated down to two digits (e.g., 03/04/49)?"

And so it was that Waldo, his friends, all good computer programmers, and I began to save those precious digits (bytes) by writing all our code using a two-digit-year format. It became common knowledge that December 12, 1948 and 12/12/48 were synonymous. And Waldo's trick would still be in vogue this very day if not for the change in the century. For we had written all of our programs to calculate dates with the following logic: if the year is 1971 (stored in the computer as 71), and you were born in 1948 (stored in the computer as 48) you are 71 minus 48, or 23 years old. What if, however, the year is 2000 (stored in the computer as 00), and you were born in 1948 (stored in the computer as 48)? Then, you are 00 minus 48 or -48 years old.

All of this brings us to our earlier equation, 00 - 48 = 52. When the dates are properly expressed (i.e., 2000 - 1948 = 52), the calculation makes sense. This is the essence of the Year 2000 hoopla—finding all of the old programs that use two-digit years and correcting them so they properly calculate dates into the next century.

Because of the magnitude and severity of this problem (it affects banking, accounting, and other critical applications), finding and correcting the two-digit years has spawned a whole new industry. Hundreds of companies are offering a combination of tools and personnel to assist organizations with their Year 2000 compliance problems. These contractors/consultants focus on finding and correcting programs (legacy code) that use a two-digit year.

To date, this effort has focused on identifying and correcting problems associated with centralized computing (i.e., mainframe applications). The identification and correction of errant code at the central computing facilities is a huge and complex initiative that will require substantial funding and resources. As large as this undertaking is, it may prove to be smaller and less expensive—while presenting less risk—than the Year 2000 issues that infect the distributed enterprise.

For a moment, let me ask you to imagine that you are charged with maintaining the health of a rhinoceros. Your responsibility is to inoculate the animal with numerous vaccines to prevent the onset of various diseases. Such inoculation includes identifying potentially harmful illnesses, administering the shots, periodically checking the animal to make certain that each vaccine is still effective, providing the proper dose (depending on size, age, gender, etc.), and ensuring the money is available to support the effort. This, metaphorically speaking, approximates the task of eradicating the Year 2000 problem within a centralized computing environment. To be certain, the task is not easy. Caution must be taken in the care and handling of the beast, and the medications are both expensive and complex to administer.

Now, imagine yourself performing the exact same task for 10,000 chipmunks that have free run of your enterprise. Here we discover new and more complex challenges, including: How do we find the chipmunks? How do we identify and distinguish such similar-looking creatures? How do we maintain accurate records on so many animals as they die, breed, etc.? How can we effectively plan the inoculation? How can we possibly maintain a schedule that allows us to be certain that the vaccine is still effective? How can we predict the cost of such a chaotic task? It is within this chipmunk metaphor that we discover the unique nature of eradicating Year 2000 problems across the distributed enterprise.

As we will see in chapter 2, an asset tracking system is an essential part of managing a Year 2000 initiative across a distributed enterprise of clients and servers. An effective asset tracking system's base functionality will tell us how many chipmunks (clients and servers) we have, indicate their current condition, and report on their movements. This critical base of knowledge is the starting point of any successful compliance effort, for it is hard to imagine fixing something you can neither define nor locate. This knowledge alone, however, will be ineffective in addressing compliance issues unless we extend its utility. It is these extensions, along with a structured methodology, that will allow us to successfully manage the enterprise toward Year 2000 compliance.

THE PLAN

So much has been said about the complexities of the Year 2000 issue that I fear I will sound foolish when making the following statement: Enterprise management of the Year 2000 effort only requires six simple steps:

STEP ONE: PROBLEM IDENTIFICATION
(CHAPTER 3)

STEP TWO: RISK ASSESSMENT
(CHAPTER 4)

STEP THREE: RISK CORRECTION
(CHAPTER 5)

STEP FOUR: COMPLIANCE PLANNING
(CHAPTER 6)

STEP FIVE: COMPLIANCE MODELING
(CHAPTER 7)

STEP SIX: RISK MANAGEMENT
(CHAPTER 8)

This process allows us to understand our risks and cost-effectively manage those initiatives that economically justify correction.

The trick to this program is that you must have the necessary information (available from asset tracking), systematically execute the steps in the proper order, and continue to "loop through" the six steps well into the next century.

In the following chapters, I address each of these steps in some detail. As I have no desire to write (and you have no desire to read) a 600-page book on this subject, I do not attempt to apply these steps to the unique attributes of each business. Rather, I rely on the assumption that readers have both common sense and a working knowledge of their businesses. Armed with these two faculties, readers should be able to project this process into the uniqueness of their business operations.

So let's see; we have an elephant under a blanket, a herd of chipmunks running amuck, all kinds of diseases, and me at a public meeting in my underwear. This is either a situation comedy, or a darned accurate representation of trying to manage a bunch of undefined problems across a distributed enterprise. If it sounds like the latter, read on.

SUMMARY

The largest things we encounter in life are not really large at all. They are but an amalgamation of tiny things that become formidable when assembled. These things are small until joined with their own kind—bricks, patriots, bacteria, votes, lies, and countless others. We must either view them en masse or lose their meaning all together.

CHAPTER 2

SMOKING HAIR

UNDERSTANDING THE BASICS

Me: *(Walking around my just-completed new home)* I'm surprised the builder didn't put a plug on the end of the dryer power line.

John (an old friend)**:** We can pick one up at the mall tonight and put it on in the morning before the movers get here.

Me: You don't think they were stupid enough to leave this line hot do you?

John: I'll go downstairs and check the box.

Me: *(Reaching into my tool belt)* Never mind. I have a power tester right here.

FLASH! POP! POP! POP!

John: *(Looking at me thrown four feet against the wall)* Are you all right? Can you hear me? What happened?

Me: *(Hair on my hands and forearms singed and smoking)* Thursday.

John: What? Do you hurt anywhere?

Me: Thursday.

It would take me several minutes to fully recover from the electrical shock I received from the 230-volt line. It would seem that I had placed the two ends of a 115-volt tester on the two hot leads of a 230-volt service, and presto! I burned the hair off my hands and forearms, and I lost most of my eyelashes. In addition, there was a black stain on my hands that would not wash off for several days.

The stain I suspect came from the vaporized ends of the tester. When the tester touched the hot wires, the bulb exploded, and the first inch of the probes vanished in the flash. In a way, I was glad my hands were stained, because it reminded me of the lesson I had learned years earlier. It was this same lesson that I tried to communicate to John, but I could only express it as "Thursday."

As I lay against the wall, stunned and unable to move, my mind seemed to be working at hyperspeed. The same thought kept repeating itself. "Understand the basics, use the right tool...understand the basics, use the right tool...understand the basics, use the right tool." This thought went through my mind with a clarity that defies description. Yet, when I tried to express it to John, all I could say was "Thursday." To this day, I do not understand why I could utter nothing but this single word; however, I fully understand both the source and the message that consumed my brain.

I first heard this profoundly simple wisdom in seventh grade. My sixth-period class that year was Wood Shop, and Mr. Silvi was the teacher. There he stood, a large African-American man with the hands of a laborer and the countenance of a professor. He looked around the room at twenty-five boys bickering to see who could sit closest to the jigsaw, and he called out his own name, "Mr. Silvi!" To fully understand the moment, you had to hear the man speak, for he had a raspy, whispery voice that sounded like it echoed through a large barrel. "Mr. Silvi," he boomed again. "That name you may or may not remember, but you will remember this...You must understand the basics and use the right tool."

Over the next year, Mr. Silvi would repeat this wisdom again and again, each time embellishing it with a broader base of understanding. By year-end, before seeing us leave his class for the final time, he would summarize it as follows: "Always understand what you are working on boys, and always pick the tool that was made to accomplish the task at hand." Then he stopped and stepped toward us; bending at the waist, he leaned forward, somehow looking directly into all twenty-five pairs of eyes simultaneously, and said, "This is not only a good work plan for your next project, it's a good work plan for your life."

It was Mr. Silvi's words that came to me as I lay stiff against that wall, arms smoking, while babbling "Thursday." Today, Mr. Silvi's words continue to course through my consciousness as I write this book about making the distributed enterprise Year 2000 compliant. It is in honor of Mr. Silvi that I write the remainder of this chapter.

UNDERSTANDING THE BASICS

It was twelve months ago that I completed my last book, *A Journey Through Oz: The Business Leaders' Road Map To Tracking Information Technology Assets.* The book explores the unique nature of managing the fragile network of desktops and servers—a network that has come to be known as the "distributed enterprise."

Within *Oz*, I discuss the risks, rewards, and the methods of proactively managing a distributed enterprise. In a brief 160 pages, I make the case that the success of most businesses is directly tied to their knowledge of their desktops and servers. This knowledge includes having a detailed understanding of each individual desktop and server (hardware, software, and configuration) and how it is changing over time.

I have no desire to repeat the information covered in *Oz*; however, the book does describe the basic functions that must be in place if you have any hope of cost-effectively managing a Year 2000 distributed compliance effort. It is for this reason that I spend the next few pages briefly reviewing the concepts of asset tracking. If you have read *Oz* and remember the primary concepts behind asset tracking, you may elect to go directly to the next chapter. If you do not have a strong working knowledge of the subject, please read the balance of this chapter before proceeding. The concepts covered in the balance of this book require a high-level understanding of the concepts and features of a full-featured asset tracking solution.

ASSET TRACKING DEFINED

Simply stated, an asset tracking system automatically gathers detailed information about every desktop and server in the distributed enterprise and stores that information in an electronic repository. The information gathered includes the hardware components, software/application components, and unique configuration settings that define each desktop and server. The specific features that define an effective asset tracking solution are covered in *Oz*. For the purpose of analyzing how to make a distributed enterprise Year 2000 compliant, we need to focus on how an effective asset tracking system functions.

OPERATION OF THE REPOSITORY

The actual operation of an effective asset tracking solution is transparent to both the end users and LAN administrators. It gathers its information automatically and stores it in the central asset repository. It is important to note that the repository contains information on all desktops and servers within the distributed enterprise. As we shall see in later chapters, the repository must have an enterprise focus, as Year 2000 compliance efforts do not lend themselves to LAN-centric management. It is not important to understand how this information is gathered. It is enough to know that the information is accurate and timely, and that it places no burden on human resources.

UPDATING THE REPOSITORY

Each time an updated view (snapshot) of the enterprise desktops is gathered, it is added to the repository. Notice I did not say that the snapshot "updates the repository." This is because the old snapshot is not discarded; instead, the repository is appended with the changes reported by the new snapshot. Typically, snapshots are taken every one to two weeks on a staggered schedule, creating minimal network load. Over time, this process provides an increasingly detailed history of each asset in the enterprise. Maintaining this comprehensive, historical base of knowledge is essential to the Year 2000 methodology outlined in this book.

USING THE REPOSITORY

Because the repository contains both current and historical information, it has multidimensional properties. Simply stated, an asset tracking system has the ability to tell you what any asset looks like at any given point in time. It also has the ability to produce a trend line on the use of a specific asset or component. In addition, because you store both past and present values for each enterprise component, you can discover missing, added, or changed attributes. This, and much more, is available as you anchor your research efforts to different aspects of the repository.

ASSOCIATIVE PROPERTIES OF THE REPOSITORY

In addition to gathering hardware, software, and configuration settings on the base of distributed assets, an asset tracking system must gather (either directly or from other enterprise solutions) associated user information. Such information includes the user name, department, physical address, phone number, general ledger code, etc. This information is associated with the hardware and software attributes that make up each specific desktop.

Within this association, we gain the ability to count things by departments and locations and compare associated trends over time. I refer to this associated information as "Phantom Comparative Anchors." As we shall see, these anchors are invaluable in addressing Year 2000 compliance issues.

ACCESSIBILITY OF THE REPOSITORY

The repository must be "open" to other applications. Technically speaking, this requires an open, relational database, enabling the repository to enrich other applications, such as help desk, fixed-asset, and compliance systems. The list of advantages of having an open repository are too numerous to cover within this context. To summarize my feelings on the subject—if you don't have an open repository, you don't have a prayer of managing the distributed enterprise.

EXERCISING THE REPOSITORY

As you can imagine, collecting multiple snapshots of data on each desktop will create a plethora of useful data. If your asset tracking system is to reach its full potential, it should provide tools that automatically convert data into actionable information. The most common tool is an easy-to-use report writer. Better systems also provide integrated analyses (such as those covered in this text) that isolate and address specific enterprise/business problems. Such problems include vendor management, Internet abuse, Year 2000 compliance, theft, etc.

In addition, an effective asset tracking system should contain an auditing component. This component allows you to define a specific condition or standard (e.g., all desktops must be running compliant versions of CalcMaster) and have the asset tracking system report (via e-mail or system alert) each time that standard is violated.

The implementation of an effective asset tracking system is more than an information technology solution. Such a system directly benefits the purchasing, finance, corporate security, help desk services, management information services, legal, and general management departments. Because of this broad application, most organizations can fully recover the cost of an asset tracking system within ninety days of deployment.

And so we move on to the defined topic, enterprise Year 2000 compliance. Those of you who have read *Oz* will no doubt feel comfortable with many of the concepts outlined in this book. Those of you who have not had a chance to read *Oz* should not hesitate to proceed, as this text stands on its own. I would, however, encourage those lacking "*Oz* credentials" to make *A Journey Through Oz* your next "enterprise read." A broad understanding of asset tracking might be the measure of difference in maintaining your sanity during the compliance process.

As we move on beyond the basics (i.e., asset tracking), we are going to assume that we have an effective asset tracking system in place. Because of this system, we have access to a base of knowledge that makes a proactive compliance effort possible. We know what our desktops and servers look like, where they are located, to whom they belong, and how they are changing over time. These are some of the basics that Mr. Silvi was speaking of when he said, "Get the basics boys. Understand what you have, get some tools, and make something." They are the basics I lacked as I pressed that tester into a 230-volt service.

Basics, however, are more than just a foundation of information. Basics identify a plan of action, a methodology to implement those actions, and a definition of required resources. It is only with these things in hand that Mr. Silvi would let us use the jigsaw, and it is only with these things that our compliance effort will be successful.

As for the tools, they are nearly inseparable from the plan because they are part of the natural flow of the compliance methodology.

Each tool we acquire will lead to new discoveries, which in turn will require a new tool. It is this effort of looping forward that will lead us to Year 2000 enterprise compliance. But enough of this academia. As Mr. Silvi would say, "Boys, sooner or later you are going to have to put hammer to nail and make something." Sounds good to me; let's take the enterprise for a spin.

SUMMARY

A problem in the hands of the ignorant is like a piano at the fingers of the untutored. It is all noise, pain, and frustration—for them, and for us.

CHAPTER 3

DINING OUT

STEP ONE: PROBLEM IDENTIFICATION

Judi *(my wife)*: It has been a really long day. Why don't we eat out tonight?

Me: *(Driving)* Great idea. Where do you want to eat?

Judi: I really don't care. You pick it.

Me: O.K., let's have Chinese.

Judi: I really don't feel like Chinese tonight. Do you mind?

Me: No problem, we can go to the barbecue place.

Judi: I had barbecue at the luncheon today...

Me: How about Mexican?

Judi: I got sick the last time we had Mexican. I just don't think I can eat Mexican.

Me: How about that little English pub?

Judi: Oh it's Saturday, and that place is always so crowded.

Me: The Italian Oven is right down the road.

Judi: I made pizza last night. Do you want Italian again?

Me: Then let's just get a burger.

Judi: If we are going to get a burger, we might as well go home and throw one on the grill. Do you want to eat at home?

Me: *(Exasperated)* Judi, where would you like to eat?

Judi: I don't care. Wherever you want to eat is fine with me.

I would like to tell you that this is a real incident that occurred only once in my life, but it is not. It is a repeated dialog that Judi and I have again and again. The names and the nationalities of the restaurants change, but the pattern is consistent. I name dining options, and they are, for various reasons, dismissed as undesirable.

This type of dialog is common to each of us. It pertains to conversations we have with our children, our coworkers, church committees, and our boss. We ask their preference, they respond with apathy, and then proceed to dismiss every option we tender as unacceptable. It would seem that they are having us chase our own tail, but this is not the case. They are not trying to frustrate us; they are merely answering a different question.

In such cases, we are making a declaration of what works, while they are defining what doesn't. And so it is with a Year 2000 compliance effort for the distributed enterprise. Those charged with the task must joyfully seek not what is desired, but what is undesirable. We, as executives in charge of such a program, must learn to speak the compliance team's language. For their victory is the discovery of a crushing problem. And when they bound in and zealously proclaim, "Guess what! We just discovered there are 11,112 desktops out there that are running a bad version of XYZ software," your response had better be enthusiastically positive. For the mission in a compliance effort is not to build or create, but to discover and clear the enterprise of buried land mines. We must keep this in mind, lest we create an apathetic team of mine searchers with low self-esteem.

One final word before moving forward. Throughout this text, I refer to problems that will surface on 1/1/2000. In a global sense, I am correct since the majority of unexpected consequences will occur on that date. At a more specific level, however, fixating on a single date of doom is misleading. Year 2000 problems can surface any time two-digit-date math is executed and one of the operations takes place on or after the Year 2000. I elect to take the poetic license of always using 1/1/2000 as a deadline in an effort to simplify the examples covered in this text.

If you keep your eyes on the news, you will see an ever-increasing list of litigation on this matter. In fact, the first Year-2000-related lawsuit has already been filed by a grocer in California. It seems that when customers use a credit card with an expiration date later than 12/31/1999, the transaction is rejected and must be manually adjusted. The grocer in question is seeking damages from the software developer. In this case, the problem surfaced two and one-half years before the turn of the century. So beware. Your first compliance issue may be closer than you think!

THE SEARCH

This mad, happy hunt for land mines is the most elemental and the most discussed aspect of the Year 2000 issue. Hundreds of firms and consulting practices have developed business units that will both help you identify at-risk applications and help you with various levels of support in making errant code Year 2000 compliant. The end product of these providers is a list of programs that have been "cracked open" and certified as either Year 2000 compliant, or corrected to be Year 2000 compliant.

Extra caution is required when contracting consulting resources. I offer one important suggestion: make certain all consulting contracts for the Year 2000 tie the deliverables back to a detailed timeline. Further, make certain sufficient financial incentives are in place to ensure that the vendor aggressively pursues meeting the dates enumerated in that timeline.

Year 2000 providers are overwhelmed with opportunities. Many of the less organized or less scrupulous providers are signing up accounts that they do not have the resources to fulfill. Protect yourself; drive your vendor toward committed dates, or you may find yourself hopelessly behind on a mission that has an immovable end point—1/1/2000. A more detailed discussion of managing vendors is contained in chapter 5.

During public speaking engagements, I often compare the identification of distributed applications that are not Year 2000 compliant to a dog chasing a car. In the case of the dog, the retort is, "Once he catches it, what is he going to do with it?" The question within the context of the distributed enterprise is, once you identify a noncompliant application, how are you going to identify the necessary fix and then make it happen? To answer this question, we must first understand the magnitude and the major points of impact of an enterprise compliance effort.

POINTS OF IMPACT

There are three primary points where the Year 2000 touches the distributed enterprise. Although the significance of each point will vary (depending upon the unique attributes of the business and enterprise), each has the potential to cause irreparable harm.

1) *In-House Developed Applications* - These are the applications that are unique to your business and were originally developed to be run from a centralized location. In most cases, as your business expanded and you responded to competitive pressures, the mainframe programs evolved to support these changes. The code was typically developed by your employees, and in many cases, has been modified to take advantage of client and server technology. These are the applications that are most often thought of as critical to your business mission, and it is for this reason that most Year 2000 consulting practices focus on this area.

The fact that many of these errant applications have been modified to take advantage of distributed clients and servers (cooperative applications) means that it is likely that they have infused their date fault into the distributed enterprise. It is logical to assume that a centralized mainframe program, which operates around a two-digit year, would require the code on the desktops and servers to calculate two-digit years as well.

Therefore, part of any effort to identify and correct errant applications on centralized processors should also include the identification of the enterprise components that are similarly affected. However, as we shall see in chapters 4 through 8, the challenge of ridding the enterprise of these "inherited problems" extends far beyond finding and correcting the errant code.

2) *Shrink-Wrapped Applications* - As more computing autonomy was granted to distributed users, organizations found themselves increasingly dependent on various commercially available applications and application suites. There are two basic types of shrink-wrapped applications. The first type runs without requiring modification, such as word processing and presentation packages. The second type depends on the end user for programming, such as spreadsheet and database applications. In many instances, these off-the-shelf products are used to support mission-critical functions.

It should come as no surprise that these shrink-wrapped applications have, over the years, undergone their own evolution. It is not unusual for the publisher of such applications to release multiple major and/or minor revisions (releases) of the software in a single year. Some users of these applications are aggressive in their migration from one release to the next. Others are prevented from migrating because the applications they developed are not compatible with later versions of the product. In fact, it is not unusual to find users who have multiple releases (versions) of a shrink-wrapped application on the same desktop.

These shrink-wrapped applications present some interesting challenges because many of them manipulate dates and, depending upon the application and the release in question, experience Year 2000 errors. The operative questions in the case of the distributed enterprise are: which applications/revisions are affected, and who is using them?

Identifying those shrink-wrapped applications and revisions of those systems that are not Year 2000 compliant requires a focused effort. You have the option of hiring an outside firm that will, for a fee, research all shrink-wrapped applications you use, and identify applications/revisions that are noncompliant. Another option is to do the research yourself. There are a number of sources you can access in this effort, including material published on the Web, periodicals, and direct contact with the various software publishers.

3) *Hardware/Firmware Compliance* - This is one aspect of the Year 2000 problem that diminishes over time. Today, there is a substantial number of older desktops and servers in the business enterprise that will incorrectly calculate dates at the change of the century. These systems will fail because their "primitives" (instructions stored on a chip within the processor) have the same two-digit-date problem as noncompliant applications. This low-level code is commonly referred to as BIOS or firmware.

Fortunately, this problem is naturally being eradicated as new processors with correct BIOS/firmware replace the older units. In addition, there are software patches that can be applied to an errant desktop or server that automatically trap and correct misrepresented dates. These patches are available free of charge from various manufacturers.

The challenge in managing this aspect of the Year 2000 issue is understanding the number of suspect machines, determining if they will still be in service on 1/1/2000, and applying the necessary patch. Within this effort, there are two means of identifying suspect machines: the gross method and the specific method. The gross method requires you to generalize the issue. For example, anything earlier than a Pentium processor is subject to Year 2000 risks, and therefore should be patched or replaced. The specific method requires you to know the production date of the BIOS/firmware in each processor and compare it to a list of those known to be noncompliant. The decision as to which method you use will depend on the turnover rate of your desktops, the availability of the appropriate BIOS/firmware list (many consulting firms are developing such lists), and resource constraints.

IDENTIFYING ERRANT APPLICATIONS

The first step in the identification of errant applications is to define the universe. The universe, in this case, contains the applications within your enterprise that deserve investigation. For example, if you have 10,000 desktops and (using your asset tracking system) you discover that you have no copies of "SmartCalc," it is unlikely that you would spend any time investigating SmartCalc's compliance status. The answer is obvious; you must first discover what you have in order to know what must be investigated.

Using an effective asset tracking system, we can produce a summary of applications that exist across the enterprise. For instance, looking at a portion of the Top Applications Analysis on the next page, we discover the most prevalent applications within the R&D department.

SUMMARY

There are 1,855 desktops (workstations and servers) in R&D and 5,603 desktops in the rest of the organization. The top 60 applications installed in R&D are listed below, as well as the following information: the application name; the percentage of R&D employees who have the application; the percentage of employees who have the application in the rest of the organization; and the difference between the percentage in R&D and the percentage in the rest of the organization.

TOP 60 APPLICATIONS INSTALLED ON R&D DESKTOPS

APPLICATION	% DEPT	% CORP	% DIFF
1) CALCMASTER V2.0	84	54	30
2) WORDSIMPLE V4.2	83	12	71
3) MAILME V1.5	82	18	64
4) GOLFWIZ V1.3	80	9	71
5) PUZZLEPRO V1.0	78	50	28
6) XL DATABASE V6.0	74	48	26
7) (LIST CONTINUES…)	…	…	…

The application that is found on the top of the list is CalcMaster, a spreadsheet application, which is installed on 84 percent of the desktops in the R&D department and on 54 percent of the desktops in the rest of the corporation. By using the Top Applications Analysis, we are able to discover those applications that make up our enterprise (define our universe of risk). With this information, we are now able to start discovering the "bad guys." This may entail hiring an outside contractor to investigate the integrity of each "enterprise-relevant application," performing your own investigation with the software publishers, or beginning a Web research effort. Most likely, you will be involved in all of the above as no one source will provide a completely satisfactory picture of your compliance exposure.

An asset tracking solution can be equally effective in discovering noncompliant hardware issues. Again, it is a matter of developing a list of the installed BIOS and investigating the compliance status of each component.

The result of the above investigation should be a list of applications and BIOS versions that are not Year 2000 compliant. Then, the logical next step is to use our asset tracking system to locate the errant desktops and make the necessary corrections. As we shall see, however, simply reacting to compliance issues in this way is both expensive and in many cases counter-productive.

While you must be certain that each problem is addressed, in some cases you may elect to live with the risk if this is the most viable solution. Before making that decision, however, other factors must be explored. For instance, you need to consider the nature and cost of the correction, the number of desktops and servers affected, the job functions of those devices, and the problem's interaction with other compliance issues.

Unlike the centralized site, where the identification and fix development is the sum of the compliance mission, such an effort within the distributed enterprise represents only a small portion of what will be required to successfully manage Year 2000 compliance. It is here that we find ourselves returning to an earlier image. We have identified all the diseases (developed a list of compliance issues), and we know where to procure the proper vaccine (understand how to correct the problem). Now comes the fun part; now it is time to wrangle the chipmunks (consider the impact on the distributed enterprise).

SUMMARY

How hard it is to remember that bad news is often our best ally. But for this pain, we might blindly walk toward certain disaster.

CHAPTER 4

• 20/20 SNOW TIRES •

Me: *(Leaving for work at 7:00 A.M. Tuesday)* I don't care how bad this snowstorm is expected to get. That's why I bought this four-wheel-drive car.

Me: *(From a phone booth at 1:00 A.M. Wednesday)* Tell your mother not to worry. I should be home within an hour.

I would first like to give myself credit where credit is due. My new Audi Quattro, with its all-weather tires, did in fact get me safely to work (the usual forty-five-minute trip took over two hours). And once arriving at the office, I worked a full day (answering phones from several hundred employees informing me they were smart enough to stay home). Further, at 6:30 P.M., my fine automobile (in spite of the eighteen inches of freshly fallen snow) successfully navigated me out of the office parking lot (it took thirty-five minutes). Now, I am not certain, but I think you have to be a male to understand that up to this point, I was feeling pretty damned good about myself.

Male hormones can only carry you so far, however, and I was about to discover their limitations as I pulled out of the office park and onto the public roads. Let me set the stage. I lived in the northern suburbs of Washington, D.C., where snowplows are used about as often (but not as effectively) as Halloween costumes. Over a foot and a half of snow had fallen, and winds were gusting up to thirty miles per hour when I had the following revelation. "Holy smoke, the other two million drivers in the greater Washington area don't own a four-wheel-drive Audi with all-weather tires!" It would seem that they failed to get the "Audi calling," resulting in their less capable cars becoming the slipping, sliding, stalling, crashing, exit-blocking, lane-obstructing, and road-closing obstacles for my silver snow-munching beauty.

It took me seven and one-half hours to get home that night, with the trek yielding some unexpected benefits. First, in my meandering trip home, I convinced myself that I got to drive every square inch of the roads in Montgomery County, Maryland. I think this has given me a fall-back career as a county planner should I ever decide on a career change. Second, I had the opportunity to help some very nice people. Although after about my thirtieth good deed, I began to wonder how many nice people I really needed in my life. Finally, I conclusively decided that I was part of something much larger, and that to truly plan my life, I had to view myself and the larger entity simultaneously.

In the same way, the assessment of how to make the distributed enterprise Year 2000 compliant requires us to be simultaneously both near- and farsighted. Each problem must be considered individually and within the context of the computing and business enterprise. Once each problem has received this treatment, all problems must be considered together to formulate an effective Year 2000 compliance strategy. The importance of viewing all problems as a whole cannot be overestimated, as most organizations will identify more issues than they have the capital and/or human resources to correct.

I know that this last statement is contrary to the wave of hysteria that pronounces nothing less than full Year 2000 compliance. The reason the Year 2000 is seen as an all-or-nothing proposition is the tremendous potential for risks. No business can ignore unquantified risk, and lacking a comprehensive assessment effort (i.e., the step covered in this chapter), businesses must target full compliance or be forced to answer some very embarrassing questions.

In addition to funding and limited resources, another reason for selective compliance has to do with the fact that the Year 2000 is an abstraction. The change in the millennium does not require consumers to buy more goods and services, nor does it mysteriously improve the efficiency of business operations. It is nothing but a date, and with the exception of those profiting from helping to solve the problem, no one is going to see revenues or profits increase as a result of this phenomenon. So where are we going to get the money to fund Year 2000 compliance? We are going to squeeze it from existing budgets and beg for increased funding as business conditions will allow. And as we beg and borrow these funds, we will be forced to compare the benefit of avoided risk to the impact of cuts and to the effect of other initiatives.

I should note that there are corporations that have been actively planning for the Year 2000 funding issue. They have been accumulating a reserve that will enable them to spread the burden of the compliance expense over a larger number of time periods. I applaud such efforts. The fact remains, however, that the bottom line will still be affected (albeit a smaller amount over a longer period), and pressure will be put on the organization not to allow such a reserve to affect earnings. Again, we return to the concept of trimming expenditures to cover the cost of the Year 2000 tab.

In an odd way, the Year 2000 initiative is also responsible for increased spending in areas that are not tied to the compliance issues. Here we discover creative managers burying pet (pork-barrel) projects into a large bucket that is labeled "compliance funds." A means of keeping such abuses in check is discussed in chapter 5.

Using the tools described in that chapter, you will be able to build a detailed budget for Year 2000 expenditures, thus making it difficult to hide unauthorized expenditures.

RISK ASSESSMENT ANALYSIS

The best way to tie all of these concepts together is to isolate a single Year 2000 problem and assess its impact. For purposes of this example, assume that you are responsible for implementing a Year 2000 compliance program for XYZ Corporation with an enterprise that is made up of 7,458 desktops. Fortunately, before beginning this effort, you read *A Journey Through Oz*, and implemented an effective asset tracking system. Using the Top Applications Analysis described earlier, you identify a widely distributed shrink-wrapped application named CalcMaster. This spreadsheet application is identified by a Year 2000 compliance certification service as being noncompliant for all releases prior to version 3.0.

Having identified CalcMaster as noncompliant, the next step is to determine its impact on the enterprise. Using your asset tracking system, you will begin by assessing CalcMaster's impact from several different perspectives. Ideally, the Year 2000 compliance module of your asset tracking system will present all of these perspectives (steps) on a single sheet. This eases the task of comparative planning (covered in chapter 6).

RISK ASSESSMENT PHASE ONE:
SUMMARY

The first phase of assessing CalcMaster is to summarize the problem. The summary on the following page is the type of information that is provided by the Risk Assessment Analysis and is required for you to move forward with the Year 2000 initiative.

SUMMARY

As of January 31, 1997, there are 1,065 days until January 1, 2000.

This analysis assumes all product releases of CalcMaster prior to version 3.0 are At-Risk. Only desktops running the MS-Windows operating system are included in this analysis.

There are 7,134 installed copies of CalcMaster on corporate desktops (workstations and servers). At-Risk desktops total 4,593. Mixed risk levels exist on 49 desktops. There are 198 desktops with Undetermined risk levels of CalcMaster. The largest number of At-Risk desktops is 1,550 in R&D. The largest percentage of At-Risk desktops is 86.6 percent in Finance.

The first thing you notice in the above summary is the Year 2000 countdown. It states that there are 1,065 days before the risk becomes reality. At first this may seem like a cosmetic nicety, but I believe every professional dealing with the millennium issue should make a habit of including the countdown on all relevant correspondence. It is this countdown, when exercised over time, that brings a concrete reality to an otherwise abstract concept.

The next section of the summary defines the risk. In this case, all versions of CalcMaster prior to version 3.0 are noncompliant, with version 3.0 and above presenting no risk. You will notice that the risk is defined around the application's version, as most Year 2000 problems are managed around versions rather than applications. This is true of both in-house developed and shrink-wrapped applications. In the vast majority of cases, you will replace an errant application with a newer one (i.e., fixed version of the same application). Therefore, when searching for noncompliant applications, you are specifically searching for the noncompliant version of the application, rather than the application itself.

The next information in the summary is the number of installed copies of CalcMaster, highlighting those versions that are at risk of noncompliance. Then the summary goes on to identify those departments that have the largest risk exposure.

RISK ASSESSMENT PHASE TWO:
NUMBER OF DESKTOPS BY RISK LEVEL

Phase two of assessing CalcMaster requires a graphical representation of the various desktop risk levels. At first, this may seem like needless repetition of information presented in the summary (phase one). Before dismissing it as redundant, however, take a moment to examine the chart.

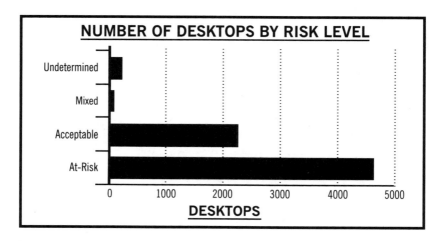

This bar chart presents the relationships between the various risk levels. The first thing we notice is that there are more than twice as many desktops with a risky version of the product than with a safe version. The second bar illustrates that there is a small number of mixed desktops (i.e., those that have both a good and bad [at-risk] version of CalcMaster). The first bar shows us the number of copies of CalcMaster that were discovered, but do not have a recognizable version number.

If we only had to deal with the CalcMaster application, the need for this graph would be minimal. Unfortunately, most organizations will find themselves dealing with dozens, if not hundreds, of "at-risk" applications. It is this chart that allows us to make our first global assessment of the problem. With just a quick look at this graphic, those responsible for Year 2000 compliance can see that further investigation is in order. Here we discover both good and bad news. The bad news is there are more than 4,500 desktops at risk, while the good news is that users appear to already be implementing acceptable versions of the application. Regardless, the graph tells us that we need to know more.

RISK ASSESSMENT PHASE THREE: RISK LEVELS BY DEPARTMENT

Knowing more about errant applications in the distributed enterprise includes knowing where the application is being used. For example, knowing that you have more than 4,500 errant copies may not be nearly as important as knowing that 1,543 at-risk copies of the spreadsheet are installed in the sales and finance departments. Spreadsheets by definition are forecasting and modeling tools, and the risk of damage from errant models in sales and finance is disproportionately high. Phase three of the assessment presents a distribution of risk by department, allowing for a qualitative, as well as a quantitative, assessment of the problem.

RISK LEVELS BY DEPARTMENT					
DEPT.	AT-RISK	ACCEPTABLE	MIXED	UNDETERM.	TOTAL
SALES	700	903	20	80	1,703
R&D	1,550	275	6	24	1,855
FINANCE	843	119	2	10	974
ADMIN	1,100	587	13	52	1,752
OTHER	400	361	8	32	801
TOTAL	4,593	2,245	49	198	7,085

RISK ASSESSMENT PHASE FOUR:
RISK DISTRIBUTION BY DEPARTMENT

In a perfect world, we would not need to worry about distributing the cost of correcting a problem to the various departments. Each department would be happy to contribute equally to ensure that their brethren in other departments are all Year 2000 compliant. Of course, in a perfect world, there would be no Year 2000 mess in the first place. Phase four of the analysis acknowledges the imperfections of the world and graphically answers the question: "Who really owns this problem anyway?" Looking at the pie chart below, it is obvious that R&D owns the majority of the problem.

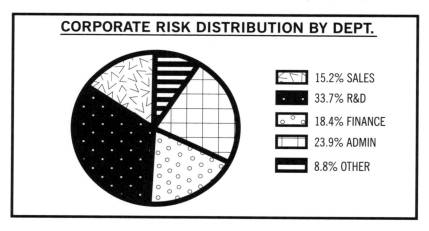

Unlike the table presented in phase three, this chart ignores those desktops that are compliant and directly summarizes errant code by department. This chart is especially useful when making a presentation to the executive of a specific department or division. These charts graphically illustrate why you are looking to them for funding and support.

RISK ASSESSMENT PHASE FIVE:
RISK LEVEL PERCENTAGE BY DEPARTMENT

A departmental focus yields yet another benefit. With this focus, we examine the dependence that a specific business unit has on the code. Phase five of the Risk Assessment Analysis presents at-risk and acceptable installations as a percentage of total desktops within the department.

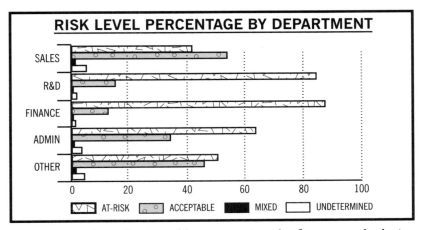

This point is best illustrated by comparing the finance and administration departments. Looking at the pie chart in phase four (page 34), we see that administration owns 23.9 percent of errant versions, while finance owns just 18.4 percent. These percentages, when considered alone, would lead to the conclusion that administration has a larger problem than finance. However, when looking at the phase five chart, we discover that while a little more than 60 percent of administration's desktops have an at-risk version of CalcMaster, more than 86 percent of finance's desktops have a fallible version of the product. This is an important fact to note given that CalcMaster is the spreadsheet of choice in both departments.

By examining finance's dependence on the application, we see the value of looking beyond the numbers alone during the compliance evaluation. Clearly, the combination of understanding that 86 percent of the desktops within the finance department are at risk and recognizing that CalcMaster is critical for finance's mission brings new questions and priorities. No doubt the finance department is at risk, and so too is XYZ Corporation.

RISK ASSESSMENT PHASE SIX:
TREND ANALYSIS

The final phase of assessing the CalcMaster risk within XYZ Corporation is to examine its presence over time. Examining problem trends allows us to anticipate and possibly alter their future. Phase six of the assessment illustrates the value of this process.

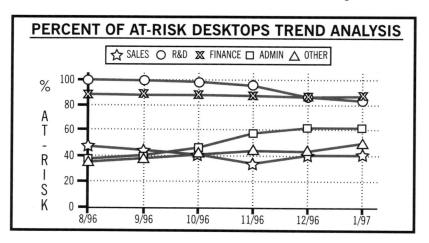

In examining this graph, we are looking for three specific opportunities:

1) *Leverage those trends that favor eradication of the problem.* Consider the trend line for R&D in the above graph. The percentage of errant copies of CalcMaster within R&D is in decline. This could be for any number of reasons that have nothing to do with the Year 2000 problem. Perhaps the department went to a new suite of office products that bundle in a different spreadsheet and CalcMaster was deleted, or maybe all new desktops being deployed incorporate a compliant version of CalcMaster. Regardless of the reason, there is an opportunity to leverage this momentum.

In this case, the first step is to inform the R&D team of their good fortune. They had a serious problem, and are on the road to fixing it. This announcement has two purposes—it informs the R&D team of the problem, and it gives you insight into the conditions that led to the positive trend. You may discover, as a result of this exchange, that over time R&D will correct the CalcMaster problem on its own. Equally likely is that R&D, being aware of the compliance issue, will make a standard of the action that led to a decline in the problem. In either case, it is possible that no extraordinary budget will need to be accumulated to address the CalcMaster problem within R&D.

2) *Immediately halt expansion of the problem.* Now consider the trend line for the administration department in the graph on the previous page. The number of errant copies of CalcMaster within administration is increasing! In this case, administration is not only increasing its Year 2000 exposure, but compounding the expense of solving the problem. Here we see a department paying for more risk (i.e., paying for more products and product installations that will do them harm). In most cases, it would cost no more to install a compliant version of the product. Again the key is to inform the department of its error. In addition, this information exchange has the added benefit of introducing departmental management to the issue of noncompliant code.

3) *Empower with knowledge.* If ignorance is bliss, then the finance department is really happy. Looking at the chart on the previous page, we see that the finance department has maintained a consistent risk level (in excess of 86 percent) for the past six months. Perhaps the corporate standard for finance includes a noncompliant version of CalcMaster, or maybe the company's desktop supplier preconfigures new desktops from an agreed-to disk image; regardless, finance is unaware of the beast it is sustaining. Informing the finance department of its CalcMaster exposure will allow its managers, at a minimum, to correct the problem on added and refreshed desktops. Again, it has the added benefit of introducing departmental management to the issue of noncompliant code.

Having completed the sixth and final phase of the CalcMaster assessment, we are now ready to consider the product's potential for harm. Ideally, these six phases would be presented on a single page as illustrated:

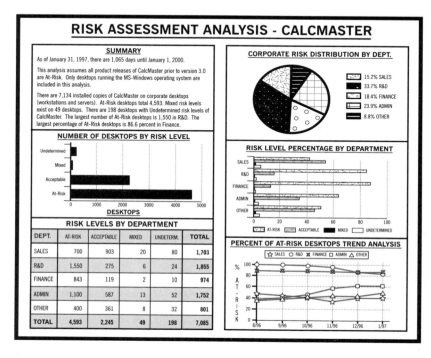

Some of what we have learned in considering the various phases of this analysis includes the following:

- In an enterprise of 7,085 desktops with CalcMaster, we have 4,593 at-risk desktops.

- Noncompliant copies of CalcMaster outnumber compliant copies by more than two to one.

- The departments that are most dependent on spreadsheets (i.e., sales and finance) have a significant reliance on noncompliant copies.

- There is a wide distribution of noncompliant versions spread throughout XYZ Corporation.

- More than 86 percent of the desktops in finance use noncompliant versions of CalcMaster.

- Several departments actually show an increasing use of a noncompliant version of CalcMaster.

Clearly, the noncompliant versions of CalcMaster present a real and substantial risk to XYZ Corporation. Before planning a strategy to address this risk, however, we need to compare it to other risks (comparative planning - see chapter 6) and put a price tag on correcting the problem (see chapter 5).

SUMMARY

There are always "others" entering the space in our lives. They converge on us and become part of the mass that defines our destiny. They will be there; it is not within our power to deny their presence. Our control rests within our vision, for we may entertain them as dance partners, or stumble over them as obstacles...that is our decision.

OYSTERS

STEP THREE: RISK CORRECTION

Me: So you're buying a horse. That's a big step.

Friend: Well, you have several horses and seem to really enjoy them. He (the horse) is a little rich for my blood, but I can afford the $2,500.

Me: Don't forget the extras.

Friend: Extras?

Me: You're going to need your own tack…you know, saddle, bridle, halter, blankets, brushes, helmet, etc.

Friend: How much you think?

Me: You could get some quality used equipment for around $1,000. Where you going to keep the beast?

Friend: I don't know yet. I thought I'd save a few bucks and look for a local farm. How much you think?

Me: About a hundred a month plus another hundred for grain, hay, and supplements.

Friend: $200 a month! Anything else?

Me: Not really, except for $100 every couple of months for shoes, maybe an average of $40-$60 per month for vet fees, $60-$75 per trip every time you haul him to a show, plus any trainer time you want to pour into him.

Friend: All this so my friends and I can ride a horse!

Me: Friends? You had better add liability insurance to the tab.

Friend: I wanted a horse. Somehow I have a feeling I'm sinking into a federal highway project.

During this dialog, my friend learned a lesson that owning a horse had taught me several years earlier. Namely, possessions are most accurately defined as a pearl surrounded by an oyster of problems. It is true that belongings do bring us pleasure; but encasing that pleasure are several challenges that must be addressed if the prize is to be held. It is for this reason that we spend most of our life discussing, agonizing over, and laughing about problems.

It is in taking care of our possessions that we find one of the certainties of our life—nothing is free. For most problems (be it your car at the mechanic, your child throwing a baseball through the neighbor's window, or a burst water heater) one must ask the next question…"What's it going to cost?" Such is the case with the CalcMaster application and with horses. We own this thing; now what is it going to cost to take care of it?

WHO PAYS FOR ENTERPRISE COMPLIANCE?

When addressing an enterprise compliance issue, you find the equally predictable follow-up question of, "Who is going to pay for it?" Someone, or some group, is going to have to find the funding to correct the problem before the turn of the century. With few exceptions, productivity gains will not be experienced as a result of bringing the application into compliance. In fact, there may even be a productivity loss. So there will be no line of people waiting to assume the burden.

The third in our predictable trio of questions is a demand for accountability. "So how much is this CalcMaster mess going to cost me?" There is a value equation at work here. What is it going to cost me? (That is, is the pearl worth the price?) So it would seem it is just a matter of dividing the cost of the corrected software proportionately and moving on with the implementation. Right? As we shall see in the remainder of this chapter, nothing could be further from the truth.

As I stated earlier, an enterprise of any size can reasonably expect to have dozens, if not hundreds, of compliance issues. If this number seems large, consider how many different spreadsheets, word processors, databases, e-mail systems, contact management systems, manufacturing systems, and in-house developed applications each department within your organization has installed. Then multiply the number of applications by the number of platforms they have (Windows 3.1, Windows 95, Macintosh, UNIX, NetWare, OS/2, DOS, etc.), and you begin to grasp the magnitude of the problem.

In addition to dealing with the sheer volume of problems, we must also cope with the complexity of a multidimensional solution. In the case of CalcMaster, for example, the new version of the spreadsheet may indeed make the software compliant, but on a certain platform, it may also require an additional 8 megabytes (MB) of main memory, 50 MB of disk space, and an operating system upgrade. If this were not enough, someone has to pay not only for these "extras," but for the installation of these additional items. All of this must be accomplished, while ensuring the entire effort will have a minimal impact on end-user productivity.

The cost-related questions surrounding Year 2000 compliance for the distributed enterprise abound. Are there funds to fix all of the identified Year 2000 problems within the distributed enterprise? If so, what is the cost of each initiative? In what order will the corrections be made, and when will funding be required? Who will pay (i.e., where is the funding coming from?) for the correction? What resources are required to make each correction? Are they available? What is the impact on end-user productivity? In most cases, it is the chief information officer, chief financial officer, or compliance executive who will have to stand before the board of directors or executive committee and answer these questions. Regardless of the messenger, the message is the same: "Here is the scope of the problem (risks), and here is how much it is going to cost to fix it."

RISK CORRECTION ANALYSIS

To give the above messenger an organized and concise picture of the funds and resources required to make the enterprise compliant, an effective asset tracking system should have the ability to generate a Risk Correction Analysis. Again, this analysis is most effective if presented on a single sheet. In addition, its utility and impact will increase severalfold if it is paired with its corresponding Risk Assessment Analysis (see previous chapter).

Unlike the Risk Assessment Analysis, which had as its sole input the targeted application and errant version information, the Risk Correction Analysis needs additional input if it is to correctly calculate the cost of problem correction. The input values are summarized in the fourth phase of the analysis (see the following illustration entitled Assumptions), but is included here, out of order, as a means of summarizing the input required to generate a Risk Correction Analysis.

ASSUMPTIONS

ACCEPTABLE RISK VERSION = **3.0**
UPGRADE VERSION = **4.0**

ELIGIBILITY

OS = **MS-WINDOWS**
SOFTWARE = **CALCMASTER**

PREREQUISITES

MEMORY >= **8 MB**
PROCESSOR >= **80486**
FREE DISK >= **20 MB**
OS VERSION >= **3.1**

COST DATA

SOFTWARE UPGRADE = **$85**
OS UPGRADE = **$40**
MEMORY UPGRADE = **$50/4 MB**
DISK UPGRADE = **$250/850 MB**
PROCESSOR UPGRADE = **$1500**
DIRECT LABOR = **$95/HR**
LOST PRODUCTIVITY = **$105/HR**

TIME REQUIRED (HOURS)

SOFTWARE UPGRADE = **3**
OS UPGRADE = **5**
MEMORY UPGRADE = **2**
DISK UPGRADE = **4**
PROCESSOR UPGRADE = **6**

The input values of the analysis (fields highlighted in bold type) were entered by the person running the analysis. This information is taken from a variety of sources. If (as in this CalcMaster example) a shrink-wrapped application is being analyzed, the Eligibility and Prerequisites answers could be on the side of the software box. The information for an in-house developed application would come from those who wrote the code. The Cost Data and Time Required are estimates that are based on past experience, or quotations from contractors. Once these values are entered, the analysis is automatically generated.

Like the Risk Assessment Analysis, the Risk Correction Analysis starts by summarizing the overall cost of correcting the CalcMaster compliance problem. The summary begins with a Year 2000 countdown and then positions the problem within the overall enterprise.

SUMMARY

As of January 31, 1997, there are 1,065 days until January 1, 2000.

There are 7,085 desktops (workstations and servers) in the enterprise running CalcMaster under Windows. Of these, 2,245 have acceptable risk levels, 49 have mixed risk levels, 198 have undetermined risk levels, and 0 do not meet eligibility requirements. No costs are calculated for these desktops. Of the remaining 4,593 At-Risk desktops, 2,550 meet the specified prerequisites and only require the new software version at a cost of $216,750. Additionally, upgrading these 2,550 desktops will result in a direct labor cost of $726,750 and a lost productivity cost of $803,250. The other 2,043 At-Risk desktops fail to meet at least one prerequisite and require an operating system and/or hardware upgrade in addition to the new software version, at a cost of $1,259,615. Additionally, upgrading these 2,043 desktops will result in a direct labor cost of $1,759,400 and a lost productivity cost of $1,944,600. The total cost of correcting all 4,593 At-Risk desktops is $6,710,365.

The summary serves several purposes. First, it is an efficient way of digesting the overall scope of a given problem because it ties together all the elements involved. The summary can also be used to educate the uninformed (e.g., department and division management) by introducing them to all of the various elements (hardware, software, labor, and lost productivity) required to correct the problem. And finally, the summary provides useful text that can be copied verbatim into the various written plans and reports that are part of the corporate planning process.

You will notice that the summary introduces a new cost element—upgrading the desktop so it can run the new (compliant) version of the application. It is sad but true that new versions of software almost always require greater computing resources. If you are to successfully plan and budget your compliance efforts, you must factor these costs into your plan. The cost of upgrading workstations that have the required computing resources to run the new versions is often a fraction of the cost of upgrading both the application and the processing platform. This summary gives us a $6,710,365 example of this premise.

RISK CORRECTION PHASE TWO: RISK CORRECTION ELIGIBILITY

Phase two of the Risk Correction Analysis focuses on risk correction eligibility.

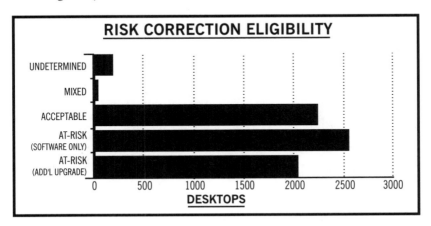

The first bar (Undetermined) highlights those CalcMaster copies that do not have recognizable version numbers. In most cases, these mystery versions are beta (yet to be publicly released) copies of the product that were supplied to the user in an effort to solve a problem. These copies can be explored further using an ad hoc report generator.

The second bar (Mixed) reflects desktops that have both compliant and noncompliant versions of CalcMaster installed. Special attention should be given to those users with two versions because some of their old applications may not run on the latest revision. Again, an ad hoc report can easily identify these users.

The most valuable bars in this phase of the analysis are the bottom three. They represent those desktops that already have a compliant (Acceptable) version of the software installed, those that only need a compliant version of CalcMaster in order to meet the Year 2000 standard (At-Risk [Software Only]), and those desktops that need additional computer components before they can accept a Year 2000 compliant version of CalcMaster (At-Risk [Add'l Upgrade]).

These three bars tell a great deal about the nature of the problems they represent. They might even be labeled "risk free," "defined risk," and "watch out!" Clearly, having a desktop that is already compliant is ideal. The next best option is just having to install a newer version of the CalcMaster software. Having to restructure the desktop with additional hardware and software upgrades, however, is both expensive and fraught with risks. It is for this reason that this phase of the analysis is ideally suited to help you define the order in which you will correct your Year 2000 problems.

Those who have limited funding in the current fiscal year may move the problems with a dominant At-Risk (Software Only) bar to the top of the stack. On the other hand, those who have a large number of At-Risk (Add'l Upgrade) applications may wish to begin with these problems, by placing them in a planned desktop refresh cycle. There are many other measures in developing a plan for enterprise Year 2000 compliance, but none does a better job of quantifying the overall risk of a specific application than this phase of the cost analysis.

RISK CORRECTION PHASE THREE:
COST BREAKDOWN

Once we understand the composition of the desktops that use CalcMaster, the next step is to understand the resources that are required to correct the problem. This is best represented in a tabular format as illustrated in phase three of the Risk Correction Analysis.

COST BREAKDOWN FOR AT-RISK DESKTOPS					
ITEM	UNITS	MATERIALS	LABOR	LOST PRODUCTIVITY	TOTAL
MEMORY	1,813	$90,650	$344,470	$380,730	$815,850
PROCESSOR	492	$738,000	$280,440	$309,960	$1,328,400
CALCMASTER	4,593	$390,405	$1,309,005	$1,446,795	$3,146,205
HARD DISK	967	$241,750	$367,460	$406,140	$1,015,350
OS	389	$15,560	$184,775	$204,225	$404,560
TOTAL	N/A	$1,476,365	$2,486,150	$2,747,850	$6,710,365

The first three columns of the table (Item, Units, and Materials) present the quantity and price of the upgrade components. The next two columns (Labor and Lost Productivity) calculate the labor expense associated with installing the materials (performing the upgrade) and the lost productivity the end users will experience as a result of having their desktops unavailable during the upgrade. It has been my experience that few people have questions regarding the first three columns of the table. The fourth and fifth columns raise the most questions, and for good reason—labor and lost productivity represent both the greatest cost and the greatest risk in most enterprise compliance initiatives.

The matter of labor would seem to be simple. Do we have the people available to do this in-house? If not, what will it cost to hire a contractor? The answer to the first question (Do we have the internal resources?) is probably no. Even if you appear to have them today, they will probably vanish as the associated burdens of Year 2000 compliance compress toward the new millennium. The fact that most information technology (IT) organizations currently have a substantial number of open job requisitions, and have had these openings for an extended period, is a strong indicator that outside contractors will be required to implement many of the Year 2000 enterprise corrections.

As almost everyone will rely on outside contractors to help address these issues, it is logical to assume there will be a shortage of such resources. This phenomenon led me to formulate the "Chris Jesse 15 percent rule." The rule simply states that it will cost 15 percent more each year to procure outside resources to address enterprise Year 2000 corrections. I believe this will continue through the Year 2000.

For example, a $100 resource contracted in 1997 will cost you $115 if contracted for in 1998, $132.25 in 1999, and $152.08 in the Year 2000. The specific percentage (15 percent) may be contested, but the logic is irrefutable. As more resources are taken out of play by earlier contracts, the price of procuring the remaining resources will rise. Add to this a strict deadline, and I think you will agree that the 15 percent estimate is perhaps modest.

How then do we contract for competent resources at an optimal price? The first step is to use your asset tracking system to produce the type of analyses discussed in this chapter. With this information, you will be able to approximate the resources required to make your enterprise compliant. Then you will have the advantage of knowing the type, location, quantity, and timing of the resources required. Using this information, you will save money in two ways. First, because you are aggregating your requirements, you will get more competitive bids. Second, because you have the information early, you will be able to avoid the 15 percent escalators.

The fifth column in the table (Lost Productivity) is perhaps the most significant element in the table. It is an estimate of how much productivity will be lost as a result of correcting end-users' desktops. I am always surprised by how little consideration mid-level IT management gives this issue, while so much interest is exhibited by upper management. Here, at least in theory, the two sets of interest should converge as the Year 2000 presents its unique demands on both internal and external resources.

As I mentioned earlier in the chapter, someone is going to have to come up with the money to pay for making the enterprise Year 2000 compliant. Often times, these funds will come from the divisions and departments that will benefit from the corrections. Now, if these business units are only presented with a cost and told to budget for the expense, they will expect to get the perfect solution for the dollars tendered. On the other hand, if they are presented with a cost and an impact on productivity, they will become more involved in an optimal solution.

An example of this principle in action is a department manager who will allow an upgrade during office hours to avoid the premium of second-shift labor. Conversely, a manager who is scheduled for an after-hours upgrade may willingly accept additional charges to avoid a hit in productivity. It is even possible that IT management and department management might agree (with training) to upgrade their own systems. All of this becomes possible when we present those picking up the tab with an itemized bill.

I do not want to leave this discussion without one more plug for considering maximized end-user productivity as the primary objective of distributed IT assets. In presenting lost productivity to departmental/division management, IT executives are acknowledging and focusing on the issues that will impact the business, and not on the chips, wires, and software of their domain. It is with this business focus that IT can have a positive cents-per-share impact on the bottom line, and the IT executives can have their rightful place in board meetings.

Before moving on to the next phase of the Risk Correction Analysis, it is useful to summarize what the analysis has already told us. Looking under the Item column at CalcMaster (see page 49), we see that the company needs to purchase 4,593 copies of a compliant version of the software. To the immediate right of the unit count, we discover the cost of that purchase to be $390,405. By using the underlying power of an asset tracking system and this Risk Correction Analysis, we discover the true cost to be $6,710,365 (lower right table entry). This may not seem like good news, but in the case of Year 2000 compliance, insightful information, not ignorance, is bliss.

RISK CORRECTION PHASE FOUR: ASSUMPTIONS

We have already seen the fourth phase of the Risk Correction Analysis (Assumptions) at the beginning of this section. I have included it again so that we might consider the accuracy of the various entries.

ASSUMPTIONS

ACCEPTABLE RISK VERSION = **3.0**
UPGRADE VERSION = **4.0**

ELIGIBILITY

OS = **MS-WINDOWS**
SOFTWARE = **CALCMASTER**

PREREQUISITES

MEMORY $>=$ **8 MB**
PROCESSOR $>=$ **80486**
FREE DISK $>=$ **20 MB**
OS VERSION $>=$ **3.1**

COST DATA

SOFTWARE UPGRADE = **$85**
OS UPGRADE = **$40**
MEMORY UPGRADE = **$50/4 MB**
DISK UPGRADE = **$250/850 MB**
PROCESSOR UPGRADE = **$1500**
DIRECT LABOR = **$95/HR**
LOST PRODUCTIVITY = **$105/HR**

TIME REQUIRED (HOURS)

SOFTWARE UPGRADE = **3**
OS UPGRADE = **5**
MEMORY UPGRADE = **2**
DISK UPGRADE = **4**
PROCESSOR UPGRADE = **6**

On several occasions, I have been asked to supply values for the above assumptions. My answer is always the same. "I have no idea what it will cost you to add 16 MB of memory to 125 desktops in Boise, Idaho—and I bet you don't either—but I bet you could guess plus or minus 10 percent to 15 percent." The point is these are estimates that allow us to frame the problem. We just discussed an example on how the expense of upgrading CalcMaster on 4,593 desktops went from a direct cost of $390,405 to an estimate of $6,710,365. Would the value of running this analysis be invalidated because the installed (actual) cost turned out to be 10 percent above or 15 percent below the six-million-dollar figure? Of course not. These assumptions are targeted at getting us in the ball park, not defining the strike zone. So take educated guesses at the values requested in the assumptions. The next phase of the analysis will detail where you need to spend your time.

RISK CORRECTION PHASE FIVE: COST DISTRIBUTION

In this final phase (phase five) of the Risk Correction Analysis, we can quickly see the relationship between the various cost components. This information is presented as a pie chart.

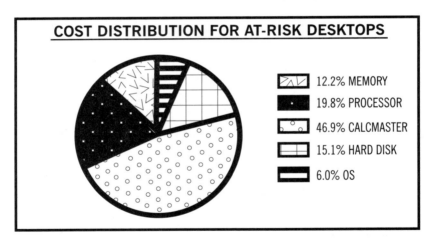

COST DISTRIBUTION FOR AT-RISK DESKTOPS

- 12.2% MEMORY
- 19.8% PROCESSOR
- 46.9% CALCMASTER
- 15.1% HARD DISK
- 6.0% OS

If you look closely, you discover that the last phase of this analysis is nothing more than a graphic representation of the total column in the Cost Breakdown table (phase three). When considering a single problem (e.g., CalcMaster), this graphic depiction is a luxury. However, as we shall see in chapter 6, it will become one of our most valued elements in developing an enterprise plan for Year 2000 compliance.

Having completed the fifth and final phase of the CalcMaster Risk Correction Analysis, we are now ready to consider how it fits into the overall compliance plan. All five phases will be important in the planning process, and having this information presented on a single page will be of immeasurable value. The sketch below illustrates a single-page presentation.

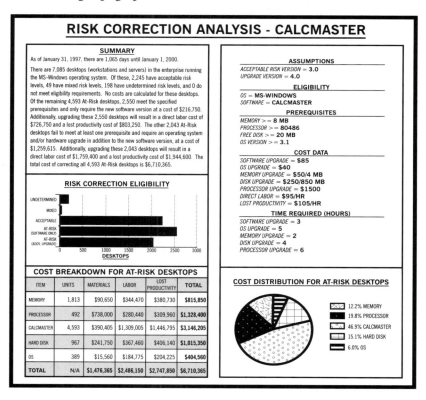

I do not want to conclude this detailed review of the Risk Correction Analysis without considering its overall utility. The Risk Correction Analysis has allowed us to quantify the CalcMaster problem in several ways. First, it has highlighted the desktops that must be restructured as part of making the application compliant. Second, it has provided senior IT management with an understanding of the true cost of making this application compliant. And finally (as we shall see in chapter 6), it provides valuable insights that will be quintessential elements in developing an enterprise-wide Year 2000 compliance plan.

SUMMARY

We need to fix this no matter what the cost!... I mean assuming it's not ridiculous...you know, if it makes sense... Just figure it out, and ah, ah...we'll talk about it.

• BURNING QUESTION •

STEP FOUR: COMPLIANCE PLANNING

My Assistant: (*Interrupting a meeting*) Chuck is on the phone, says he needs to talk to you.

Me: Did you tell him I am in a meeting? I can't leave now. Tell him I will come to his office as soon as I am done.

My Assistant: He says he's out at a customer site.

Me: Well get the number and I will call him back.

My Assistant: I tried, but he's calling from a phone booth.

Me: I am right in the middle…ask when I can call him at the customer's office?

My Assistant: (*Returning to the meeting room*) He said he'll have to ask the fire marshal.

Me: What? Just tell him I will wait for him here, and to get back as soon as he can.

My Assistant: (*Again returning*) He wants to make sure that you don't want him to stay with the evidence.

Me: (*Leaving the meeting*) Put him through to my office.

At the time, I was the executive in charge of a business unit for a large company that manufactured computers. Chuck was a senior customer service technician who, because of his considerable skill, drew the more difficult assignments. The meeting in question was a budget-planning affair where my senior managers were in a heated debate as to the merits of their newly assigned objectives.

Now those of you who have been responsible for assigning goals and budgets know that the trick to managing such a meeting is to treat it like an aggressive dog. You pay attention, don't run, and appear fearless. On this day, I was at the top of my game. The meeting was three hours old and, although heated, I had managed to focus my every thought on moving the process forward. I was doing well, and to be honest, was a little irritated that Chuck's messages kept demanding my attention.

Chuck's first interruption was the call itself. He was an exceptional technician, and his placing the call was significant. Then there was the somewhat unusual calling from a phone booth at a customer site, a conversation with a fire marshal, and finally the "evidence." No one of these issues could have penetrated my iron curtain of focus and drawn me out of that meeting. It was only when these little yellow sticky notes were arrayed in force that Chuck got my attention and interrupted the meeting.

I've learned that the process I went through in prioritizing Chuck's call is a part of the human condition. Although there may be a psychological term for it, I call it "relative understanding." This phenomenon is nothing more than gathering facts together and considering them as a whole. It is in this process of associating one fact with another that new understandings emerge.

For example, when my eighteen-year-old daughter Rachel (a college freshman away from home for the first time) informed my wife and me that a young man in the dance department had been attentive and helpful, I was grateful that she was making friends. However, when my wife later contributed the newly discovered fact that he was a thirty-one-year-old teaching assistant, my view of this college "friend" shifted toward "dirty old man."

Having completed the first three steps (Identification, Assessment, and Correction), we are ready to begin planning a Year 2000 compliance program for the distributed enterprise. The next step is to apply the concept of relative understanding to our CalcMaster example. To quickly review, we know what the problems are, how they affect the enterprise, and what it will cost to fix them. At this point, we have an isolated understanding of each problem (i.e., the suspect application alone modeled against the enterprise [comparative planning]). As we shall see, having these "isolated pictures" of problems will be invaluable in the first part of our planning process. This, however, is only the first step, for there is also the need to view them within the context of relative understanding. It is with this effort that we discover how these problems interact with one another, as well as how they interact with the logistics of the business.

Before moving on to a detailed discussion of the planning process, let me clear up a few loose ends. Chuck's problem with the fire marshal had to do with a computer cable that had overheated and began to smoke as the insulation melted. The problem was isolated and corrected. No one was injured. As for the teaching assistant, he was actually just a caring, concerned member of the faculty whose only interest was helping young students. NOT! He was a dirty old man. The situation was corrected.

SORTING OUT THE PROBLEM

For the moment, assume that you are in charge of an enterprise that is built around a strong corporate desktop standard (corporate standard enterprise). Within this enterprise, you have identified forty noncompliant applications. Further, you have run a Risk Assessment Analysis and Risk Correction Analysis for each. Now what? The answer involves a roll of two-sided removable tape and a large blank wall. (WARNING! Make sure you have two-sided **removable** tape as I have discovered that the property management people get pretty testy when you start peeling off the wallboard.)

You are now going to take the first of our props and place a piece of tape on the back of each Risk Assessment Analysis. You should have a separate Risk Assessment Analysis for each of the forty non-compliant applications you identified. Then place them on the wall in three groups: Priority Applications, Important Applications, and Other Applications. Do not spend a lot of time doing this as (I hope) you are using removable tape, and these sheets will be reordered any number of times as we work our way through the planning process. At this point, you should have a wall that looks like the following diagram.

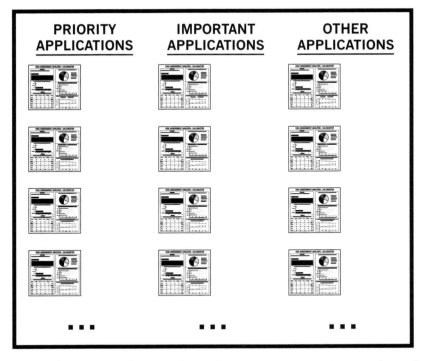

Depending upon the specifics of your enterprise, the number of applications and the distribution of their priorities will vary. The important thing is to get them all posted on the wall since less important compliance issues may receive an elevated priority as we proceed with the planning process. You will also notice that there are spaces between each chart, enabling us (later in the planning process) to post the corresponding Risk Correction Analysis next to each of these assessments.

You now have the sum of your enterprise compliance effort before you, and you have sorted each application by perceived priority. You will no doubt reorder these using one, or a combination of, rating factors. Some of these factors include:

• The gross number of desktops affected.

• The ratio of compliant to noncompliant desktops.

• The nature of the application as it relates to its departmental distribution (e.g., spreadsheets are very important to finance).

• How widespread the problem is across the corporation. Is it an isolated departmental issue or does it have broad corporate impact?

• The depth of risk assumed by each department. Perhaps a problem gets priority because it is present on 90 percent of the machines in R&D and finance, even though the overall number of desktops affected within the enterprise is not significant.

• The problem trend. A problem that affects a large number of desktops, but has a steep decline in use, may deserve a lower priority than a problem affecting fewer desktops with an increase in use.

There are, of course, other rating factors, some of which are unique to your organization. All of these would be used to reorder the sheets on the wall before considering the cost component of the planning process. You should now have three categories of problems before you: Priority Applications, Important Applications, and Other Applications.

Within each category, the applications should be prioritized from most important to least important. Now before adding the corresponding cost sheets to the wall, you should label each sheet with its category and priority within that category (i.e., P1, P2, P3, I1, I2, O1, O2, etc.). This will help you remember the initial priorities you assigned the application as you reorder them based on cost considerations.

Placing the Risk Correction Analyses on the wall next to their corresponding Risk Assessment Analyses gives us a new vision of how enterprise compliance might be ordered (see below).

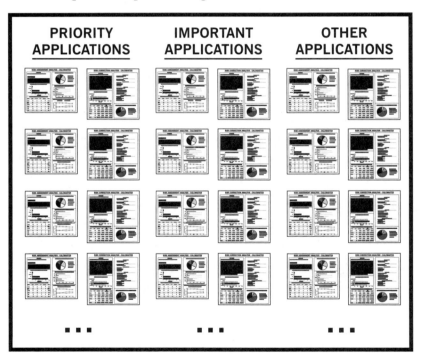

Some of the aspects that may come to light with the supporting cost information include:

- *Budget constraints* - Your number-one-priority item may be too expensive to be addressed in the current fiscal year, and therefore may need to be moved down in priority to a future fiscal budget.

- *Limited resources* - Resources, both internal and external, may not be available to perform aggressive upgrades of the enterprise. This may require you to give greater priority to those compliance issues that are predominantly software-only upgrades.

- *End-user productivity concerns* - The cyclical nature of your business may be in conflict with your correction priorities. For example, if a specific compliance problem has a high lost productivity factor, and you are in the retail business, it is unlikely (regardless of other concerns) that you would schedule this compliance initiative for the fourth or first calendar quarters (holiday season).

- *Efficiencies* - Certain compliance initiatives may overlap. For example, if 90 percent of the desktops in the finance department need CalcMaster (a high priority), and 75 percent of the desktops in finance need a new version of calendar management software (a low priority), then, because of installation efficiencies, the calendar management software might be joined to CalcMaster on the high-priority list.

- *Budget distribution* - As mentioned earlier, the money to correct the Year 2000 compliance problem must be extracted from existing budgets. When specific departments or divisions will directly fund the correction of their desktops, it may be necessary to bend priorities around budget availability. Therefore, a lower-level problem that has funding may get priority over a higher-priority problem that has no funding.

- *Critical mass of upgrade activity* - Perhaps a significant number of desktops require an operating system upgrade in order to run compliant applications. This might prompt an investigation of any additional components required to support the operating system upgrade. This information is included in the lower right-hand corner of the Risk Correction Analysis (shown on the next page).

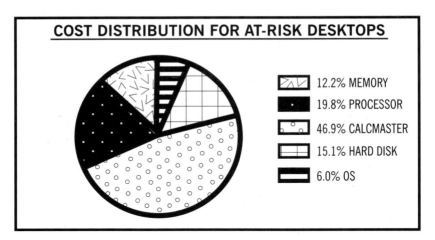

COST DISTRIBUTION FOR AT-RISK DESKTOPS

12.2% MEMORY
19.8% PROCESSOR
46.9% CALCMASTER
15.1% HARD DISK
6.0% OS

You may discover that several of your top-priority desktops require a processor upgrade. You may want to search for these so they can receive application and component upgrades during a single effort.

CONSIDERING ORGANIZATION-SPECIFIC AND AUTONOMOUS ENTERPRISES

Depending on the complexity of your compliance initiative, your corporate structure, and the level of standardization that exists within the enterprise, the above prioritization process may be all that is required to develop an efficient and cost-effective compliance program. There are, however, two conditions in which the above prioritization process may not be fully effective. Notice that I did not say ineffective, as you would still be wise to use this methodology as a starting point. These two areas, organization-specific enterprises and independent enterprises (enterprises that give their users a significant degree of autonomy), share a common denominator—complexity.

The definition of an organization-specific enterprise varies, but here we will define it as a company or public institution that goes to extremes in setting up autonomous IT functions within the various departments, divisions, etc. These functions form a loose alliance with those responsible for the centralized processing and the communications infrastructure (CIO) to form what I like to call a "confederation of anarchy." This is a reasonably peaceful kingdom until something goes wrong, at which time everyone screams for action and points their finger at the CIO. It is in this type of environment that an extra step must be taken when setting priorities for Year 2000 compliance.

This extra step is actually a repetition of the priority-setting process, except that it drills down to the individual business units. You would still go through the exercise of examining and setting priorities for the enterprise as a whole, as this information is necessary for optimum component pricing and for optimal terms with outside contractors. Once this is complete, however, the next step is to use your asset tracking system (this assumes you have an asset tracking system with an open database, see chapter 2) to create a unique view of the repository that contains only those desktops in a specific department, division, etc. With this view in place, you then run the same Assessment and Correction Analyses and create organization-specific prioritization of the Year 2000 compliance issues.

Using this technique, you can generate a Year 2000 plan that appeals to the parochial interests of the various business units, and introduce them to the broader concept and cost benefits of viewing Year 2000 compliance from an enterprise perspective.

The value of organization-specific enterprise perspectives extends beyond keeping the various kingdoms at peace. Unique views can also be created for specific processing platform types (UNIX, Macintosh, NetWare, Windows, etc.), geographic locations, and job functions. These views can be of great value when planning compliance rollout and when proactively managing labor and travel expense.

The autonomous enterprise, either by design or accident, is a complexity of complexities. This enterprise has evolved, and contains a wide variety of platforms, running a diverse set of applications that conform to a multitude of standards. Now before sounding like I am down on this structure, let me say that when it is working, it provides for optimum user productivity. It is this type of enterprise that you will find in my own company. It does not come without a price, however. For when it is time for a coordinated enterprise-wide effort (e.g., Year 2000 compliance), it is akin to getting our herd of chipmunks to perform *Swan Lake*. I know that getting chipmunks to perform a ballet may sound impossible, but if you can find enough little tiny costumes, give them the right incentives, and find an appropriate stage, you may be surprised by what you can accomplish.

Simply stated, the problem with making an autonomous enterprise Year 2000 compliant is the number of variables. The creativity that has allowed the various departments and users to develop an optimal work environment has also generated a large number of compliance problems across a wide variety of platforms.

Consider our earlier example of forty problems posted on the wall. What if you had the same forty problems, but four different platforms to contend with? Each platform would have a unique compliance target for CalcMaster and every other application listed on the wall. A single compliance strategy for CalcMaster is no longer adequate. We now need a compliance strategy for CalcMaster-Macintosh, CalcMaster-Windows, CalcMaster-DOS, and CalcMaster-UNIX. Assuming that each of our forty problems was deployed on an average of two platforms, our compliance list would increase to eighty.

At the same time the autonomous enterprise is bringing the added complexity of multiple platforms, it is also introducing a much larger number of compliance issues (applications). Our initial response is, "The user (department/division) selected the application. Now let the user figure out what is noncompliant, and how to fix it." Regardless of our feelings, it is the corporate entity that will ultimately realize the risk and suffer the consequences of a noncompliant application. It is for this reason that enterprise Year 2000 compliance should be addressed from a corporate or enterprise perspective.

Going back to our earlier example, if we substitute an autonomous enterprise for the earlier-defined corporate standard enterprise, we can expect compliance problems to increase from forty to more than 160 issues. If this seems unreasonable, consider the following two conservative assumptions. One might expect an autonomous enterprise to have at least twice as many "mission-critical" applications as an enterprise that operates around a strong corporate standard. Second, an autonomous enterprise supports a greater variety of platforms and, therefore, can be expected to average no less than two platforms per application. That would be two times the number of applications found in the corporate standard enterprise (40 * 2), times the earlier-discussed average of two platforms per application (80 * 2), and you reach a very plausible 160 compliance issues. Using the priority-setting methodology will require us to either locate a very large wall or group the compliance issues among common attributes (cases).

This seemingly unmanageable tangle of applications, organization units (e.g., departments), platforms, time frames, and budgets can be managed if we think of them in terms of "cases." A case is nothing more than a grouping of noncompliant applications around some common factor(s). A case might simply consist of all compliance problems that can be fixed in the entire enterprise and do not require any hardware or operating system upgrades. Or a case can be specific and consist of all business applications on UNIX desktops in the engineering department that fall within this year's fiscal budget. The dominant and recessive factors to consider when developing your cases largely depend on the specifics of your business and the makeup of your enterprise. There is one factor, however, that should always be part of any case creation, and that factor is timing.

The importance of timing can best be illustrated by example. Suppose you have a group of desktops that are running Windows 3.1 and require a CalcMaster upgrade. You isolate those workstations, procure the correct number of copies of compliant software, procure and install the necessary desktop hardware and operating system upgrades, and implement the compliant version of CalcMaster. Later, you initiate a program to make your word processor (WordGreat) Year 2000 compliant. Now assume for a moment that there is a 75 percent overlap between the desktops that received the CalcMaster upgrade and those that will receive the WordGreat fix. Here we discover the value of timing. Since the compliant version of WordGreat only runs under Windows 95, each desktop receiving the new WordGreat will also be required to run Windows 95. The problem is that the compliant version of CalcMaster you installed earlier will not run under Windows 95. You will now be required to fix your CalcMaster correction by installing a Windows 95 version of the CalcMaster application. This in turn may spawn yet another hardware upgrade of certain desktops.

The issue of timing applies to hardware as well as application compliance. An application that requires a 4 MB upgrade, if installed before an application that requires an 8 MB upgrade, would both double the installation cost of the memory, and potentially obsolete the 4 MB component. Disk space also deserves timing considerations because the additional hard drive added to the various desktops should be the sum of all compliance requirements. There is little value in upgrading the hard drive on a desktop to accommodate the first application only to require another upgrade later. With this in mind, it is logical to always consider the timing of upgrade compliance issues when constructing your compliance plans. This also leads us to compliance modeling, which is discussed in chapter 7.

As you go through the iterative process of compliance planning for your enterprise, the ad hoc reporting capabilities of the asset tracking system will be invaluable. An effective reporting system will allow you to develop lists that locate desktops that meet certain criteria and combinations of criteria. For instance, you can identify all desktops with only 4 MB of memory running Windows 3.1. Using these lists you will be able to construct logical cases of corrections and execute those cases in a proper sequence.

SUMMARY

He was a horrid human being, ill mannered, uneducated, dirty, and foul of odor. He was in all ways repugnant, save one thing: he alone knew the way. Somehow this, relatively speaking, made him a fine companion.

CHAPTER 7
• DINOSAUR FEATHERS •
STEP FIVE: COMPLIANCE MODELING

Mike (a childhood friend): *(Dropping a new engine in his English Ford)* I just can't figure out how to cable this through the fire wall. I called Vince *(local mechanic)* and he said he would stop by.

Me (sixteen years old): So once you get her running, what do you think she'll do?

Mike: Hard to tell, but she'll have over twice the horse power and three times the torque.

Vince: *(Arriving)* Hey Mike. Let me take a look. Where's the new wiring harness?

Mike: *(Handing him the part)* This is the last step, get this done and we are crrrruising…

Vince: You know, Mike, you did a real fine job putting this great big engine in this little tiny car, but I don't think you should actually drive it.

Mike: What?

Vince: Mike, you rev this thing up and you're going to blow up the exhaust system and tear out the transmission…and besides, you don't have the brakes to hold this thing down.

Mike: What are you saying?

Vince: Mike, what you have here is a dinosaur with a hummingbird ass...you may get her started, but once she gets going it's not going to be pretty.

Although I was hesitant to use Vince's graphic description of Mike's car (in fear that the language might be offensive), I opted to leave his wisdom unchanged. "A dinosaur with a hummingbird ass." I can think of no words that more precisely describe the condition of Mike's car, or in some cases, our compliance effort. For Mike had assembled a set of working systems, each of which connected and functioned to specifications. The problem—the components were not complementary—resulting in a fatal design flaw.

I recount this lesson, taught to two sixteen-year-old boys by a wise mechanic, as a means of introducing the value of compliance modeling. I entertain this discussion with certain reservations. All of the tools and systems I have covered thus far are available today in an asset tracking system with a comprehensive Year 2000 compliance module. It has consistently been my practice, when writing books and articles, to avoid discussing concepts that are not commercially available. I believe this is especially important when discussing Year 2000 solutions where great ideas seem to outnumber practical solutions by an order of magnitude. I have no doubt these "idea providers" have the best of intentions, but intentions do not make an enterprise compliant, and with the clock ticking, false starts are doubly painful.

My apprehension is outweighed by the benefits of the Compliance Modeling tool:

1) This tool is a natural extension of asset tracking technology; thus, much of what is required is already in production.

2) At the time of this writing, the module is imminently available.

3) This tool has the potential to have a major positive impact on the cost, accuracy, and timeliness of our distributed enterprise Year 2000 compliance initiatives.

Simply stated, a Compliance Modeling tool allows you to avoid compliance design flaws by modeling compliance efforts before they are implemented. A Compliance Modeling tool takes as its input the applications that you already examined in the Risk Correction Analyses. For example, we already generated a Risk Correction Analysis for the CalcMaster application. That analysis showed us that installing 4,593 copies of CalcMaster would cost more than $6.7 million in material, labor, and lost productivity. For a moment, assume that you ran a similar Risk Correction Analysis for twenty-five other applications named Application B through Application Z.

Specifically, a Compliance Modeling tool allows you to build a case by selecting any combination of these previously run Risk Correction Analyses, and it produces a listing of how each desktop must be modified to optimally satisfy that combination of compliance issues. The Compliance Modeling tool automatically eliminates redundant upgrades, totals the required resources across the applications defined in the case, and flags applications that introduce compliance conflicts such as incompatible operating systems.

To better illustrate this concept, I have constructed a simplified four-column example on the following page. Column A is a list of prerequisites contained in the Risk Correction Analysis. Column B contains CalcMaster's specific prerequisite components for each item listed in Column A. Column C contains the same information for the WordGreat application. Finally, Column D is the model's projected requirement for our hypothetical user (John Smith).

FOR USER JOHN SMITH			
COLUMN A	COLUMN B	COLUMN C	COLUMN D
ITEM	CALCMASTER	WORDGREAT	MODEL
MEMORY	+4 MB	+8 MB	+8 MB
PROCESSOR	N/A	N/A	UNCHANGED
CALCMASTER	CALCMASTER 3.3	N/A	CALCMASTER 3.3
WORDGREAT	N/A	WORDGREAT 4.2	WORDGREAT 4.2
HARD DISK	+30 MB	+65 MB	+850 MB
OS	N/A	WIN 95	ERROR***

***Case applications specify conflicting operating systems.
See the assumptions information in the specific correction analyses.

Let's briefly walk through the logic of the model:

Row 1 (Memory) - The model reveals that the CalcMaster Risk Correction Analysis has determined that John Smith's current configuration is inadequate and needs an additional 4 MB of memory (Column B) in order to run the compliant version of CalcMaster. It also discovers from the WordGreat Risk Correction Analysis that John's current configuration requires 8 MB of additional memory (Column C). The model recognizes that the memory increase required for running WordGreat will more than meet the memory needs of CalcMaster and so ignores the 4 MB CalcMaster requirement (Column B) and projects an 8 MB memory upgrade for John Smith's machine.

Row 2 (Processor) - As neither the CalcMaster nor the WordGreat Correction Analysis indicated that a processor upgrade was required, the model labels the processor unchanged (Column D).

Row 3 (CalcMaster) - The CalcMaster Risk Correction Analysis shows that John Smith requires a new copy of CalcMaster version 3.3 (Column B). The WordGreat Risk Correction Analysis obviously does not identify CalcMaster as being necessary for WordGreat and shows no requirement (N/A in Column C). The model projects a need for CalcMaster version 3.3.

Row 4 (WordGreat) - This is the same situation as described in row 3 except WordGreat is examined.

Row 5 (Hard Disk) - The CalcMaster Risk Correction Analysis indicated that John Smith's current desktop configuration requires an additional 30 MB of disk space to accommodate the correct version of CalcMaster (Column B). The WordGreat Risk Correction Analysis indicated that 65 MB are required (Column C). In this case, the model totaled both requirements (95 MB), compared it to the disk upgrade unit specified in the Risk Correction Analysis (850 MB), and determined that a single unit of the specified disk upgrade unit was sufficient to meet both application requirements (Column D).

Row 6 (Operating System) - In this case, the Risk Correction Analysis determined that no change in John's desktop was required to run the compliant version of CalcMaster (Column B) as John was already running the required Windows 3.1 operating system, which was the requirement in the Risk Correction Analysis. The WordGreat application, on the other hand, needs Windows 95 (Column C) to run its compliant version. The model in this case flags an error. This is an example of including applications in a case that has conflicting requirements (i.e., mismatched corrections). Those seeing this result have the option of finding a compliant version of CalcMaster that runs under Windows 95, or a compliant version of WordGreat that runs under Windows 3.1.

The above example focuses on a single user, John Smith. The primary value of a Compliance Modeling tool, however, lies not in analyzing a single user, but in having the opportunity to experiment with various scenarios without risking materials, scarce implementation resources, or lost productivity. The system then goes on to present a detailed plan as to how each desktop must be modified to achieve the desired result. Please note that the table on the following page is illustrative and is not the actual output you would receive from the Compliance Modeling tool. Much more detail would be included in an actual report, including the user's address, location, department, phone number, required modifications, costs, etc. Depending on the task at hand, this information might be presented in a number of different formats.

The true power of a Compliance Modeling tool is best viewed in a larger scale. Consider our earlier example of an enterprise with 7,458 desktops. What if you wanted to develop a plan to make the "standard business applications" compliant across the enterprise (e.g., a Business Tools - Enterprise Compliance Case)? From your identification and assessment steps, you know that the enterprise uses four different word processors, two different spreadsheets, three e-mail systems, and four desktop database systems that are not Year 2000 compliant. Having run a Risk Correction Analysis on each of these thirteen applications has given you an understanding of the time and resources required to individually address each problem. Now, you are creating a "case" that will assess the impact of correcting these applications as a single initiative.

Using the methodology described earlier, the Compliance Modeling tool would produce a report on each user (desktop). A sample of such a report is illustrated on the facing page.

CASE - BUSINESS TOOLS - ENTERPRISE COMPLIANCE
MODEL CREATION DATE - 10/02/1997 • 09:23:15

DESKTOP PROFILE

USER NAME - **JOHN SMITH**
DEPARTMENT - **FINANCE**
ADDRESS - **PEACHTREE CORPORATE BUILDING**
               1111 SILICON CTR. DRIVE
               ATLANTA, GA 30076
               SUITE 500
LOCATION - **MAIL STOP 4W313**
PHONE - **(770) 851-1234 EXT. 848**
NETWORK ADDRESS - **3567834**
ASSET ID - **254386D**

DESKTOP CONFIGURATION • 10/02/1997
(RECOMMENDED CORRECTION)

PROCESSOR - **486**
MEMORY - **8 MB (+8 MB)**
DISK CAPACITY - **250 MB (+850 MB)**
AVAILABLE DISK - **14 MB**
OS - **WINDOWS 3.1 (ERROR)*****
WORDGREAT - **VERSION 1.8 (VERSION 4.2)**
WORD ADVAN - **NA**
WORDWORLD - **NA**
BASIC WORD - **NA**
CALCMASTER - **VERSION 2.1 (VERSION 3.3)**
SPREADPAC - **NA**
MAILME - **VERSION 1.5 (VERSION 2.0)**
BETTER MAIL - **NA**
FAST MAIL - **NA**
XL DATABASE - **VERSION 3.8 (VERSION 6.0)**
DB SIMPLE - **NA**
YOUR DATA - **NA**
DATA BASE-IC - **VERSION 1.7 (VERSION 1.9)**

****Case applications specify conflicting operating systems.*
See the assumptions information in the specific correction analyses.

A similar report would be prepared for each of the thousands of desktops that meet the case criteria. In addition, the asset tracking system could run a unique view of this case. For example, the Business Tools - Enterprise Compliance Case (current example) with a restricted view might become the Business Tools - Finance Compliance Case or the Business Tools - Baltimore Compliance Case. In using the various views that can be defined by a comprehensive asset tracking system, you can address both organizational and logistical issues when planning your compliance efforts.

Of course, a comprehensive Compliance Modeling tool would also generate summary information on each case. Such a summary would detail (for the group of applications and the view selected for the case) the quantity of materials (hardware and software) required, the cost of those materials, total projected labor costs, and total lost productivity costs.

It should be noted that cases are not static. Assuming you have just run the "Business Tools - Enterprise Compliance Case" and reviewed the detail and summary information, you would then have the opportunity to modify and rerun the case. You would certainly want to resolve the operating system conflict contained in the example, but you may also want to add or delete an application from the case in an effort to meet budget objectives, optimize implementation resources, and/or control lost end-user productivity.

I think you will agree that a comprehensive Compliance Modeling tool is an invaluable tool in cost-effectively bringing your enterprise into compliance. I caution you that this tool is best used at the end of the compliance effort. That is, you must complete the first four phases (Risk Identification, Risk Assessment, Risk Correction, and Compliance Planning) before Compliance Modeling can be effectively employed.

I would argue that this four-phase methodology should be used regardless of the availability of Compliance Modeling technology. Granted, it might take five times the effort to produce a fraction of the results, but similar modeling is possible using a combination of a good report generator, SQL (structured query language) statements, a spreadsheet, and a lot of labor. Even with these inefficiencies, this "manual compliance modeling" is still supremely efficient when contrasted against the mistakes that would be made should such a methodology not be employed. In short, hopefully you can buy it; but, if not, build it. In any case, use it!

SUMMARY

Our imagination is one of God's greatest gifts. It is a mental laboratory, allowing us to discover problems before they are encountered, opportunities that masquerade within the routine, and dreams that may yet be possible.

CHAPTER 8

PONY LEGS

Me: *(In the kitchen)* Go out and get your pony. I want to see how that cut on the back of her leg is healing.

Amanda (my seven-year-old daughter): Where do you want me to put her?

Me: Just out by the driveway, near the barn. I'll be there in a minute.

Mary (my older daughter): *(Looking out the back window, five minutes later)* Dad, Bejou *(Amanda's pony)* is in the backyard grazing in the vegetable garden.

Me: *(Screaming from the kitchen)* Amanda!

Amanda: *(From the family room)* Yes sir?

Me: Didn't I tell you to take your pony out of the field and put her next to the driveway near the barn?

Amanda: Yes sir.

Me: Well she's eating the plants in the garden.

Amanda: I did what you told me. I left her there five minutes ago. Did I do something wrong?

Funny thing about chores, some of them kind of wait around for you to complete them, while others have a mind of their own and find their way to the vegetable garden. As Amanda discovered, her chore fell into the latter category, and as we shall discover, our effort to make the enterprise Year 2000 compliant is vegetable-garden-bound as well.

How can this be? It would seem that we have completely surrounded the topic of making the enterprise Year 2000 compliant. We have identified the errant applications, assessed their impact on the business and technology enterprise, calculated and isolated the various costs, and developed a rational and attainable implementation plan. Assuming we have an effective program to procure the necessary materials and resources, all that is left is to install the necessary corrections. Sounds good, except for one thing…this pony has legs.

The "legs" I speak of are the natural movements that occur within the enterprise. During the time when compliant corrections are being rolled out to the enterprise, business units will continue their normal commerce. This includes expansion, downsizing, reorganizations, management changes, and more. In addition, both individuals and operating units will react to the changes that Year 2000 compliance brings to their desktops. Using our CalcMaster spreadsheet example, let's examine some of the types of movement that may be detrimental to your Year 2000 compliance initiative.

In this example, assume that on January 1, 1997 (the date of all of the earlier-discussed analyses) you formulated and began implementing a plan that would make all copies of CalcMaster compliant by 9/30/1999. Because of budget constraints, this was a phased plan that included ordering all new desktops with the correct version of CalcMaster, as well as bundling a correct version of CalcMaster with a correction of a major in-house financial system. In the latter case, any desktop that received the new version of the in-house developed system and had a noncompliant version of CalcMaster installed would receive both the correct in-house application and correct version of CalcMaster. The remaining CalcMaster at-risk desktops (those neither upgraded nor bundled) would receive a CalcMaster upgrade on a predetermined schedule, resulting in full compliance on 9/30/1999. Comfortable with your CalcMaster compliance plan, you spend the next six months working on other compliance issues.

As I said earlier, the enterprise has legs; it has a certain life and rhythm of its own. In the six months that passed, several external events occurred that negatively impacted the CalcMaster compliance plan. These included:

- A core group within the finance department discovered that one of their more complex CalcMaster spreadsheets did not run under the new version of the product, so they reinstalled the old version.

- A small firm was acquired during the first half of the year, adding 480 new employees and 290 copies of noncompliant versions of CalcMaster to the enterprise.

- Ninety marketing employees, who were having trouble with their office suite applications, received a patched copy of the suite product that allowed them to complete their assigned task. Unfortunately, the patched version of the suite reinstalled a noncompliant version of CalcMaster.

- Frank Edwards in the consulting group developed, on his own time, a clever spreadsheet that takes input from the billable-hours application and automatically generates a nearly complete expense report. Frank makes his spreadsheet available to the other eighty-five consultants and informs them where they can purchase an inexpensive (noncompliant) copy of CalcMaster. Over half of the consultants avail themselves of Frank's offer.

I could continue giving examples, but I think I have made my point. The enterprise changes—for reasons that make sense or are stupid, for reasons that are highly visible or invisible, the enterprise will change. The question is, within the context of our Year 2000 initiative, how will we manage that change? The answer is found in the final step of a Year 2000 compliance system, Risk Management.

RISK MANAGEMENT ANALYSIS

The Year 2000 component of an effective asset tracking system should provide a means of managing the compliance plan for each application that is at risk. This component should provide an analysis that both tracks the compliance effort to date and projects future efforts required for full compliance. Ideally, such an analysis would appear on a single page making it easy to post and compare progress over time.

There are six phases in an effective Risk Management Analysis. Before presenting the specifics of this analysis, however, let me set the stage. As you recall, back in January 1997 we ran Assessment and Correction Analyses for the CalcMaster application. Using these analyses, we developed a plan that would allow us to make CalcMaster enterprise compliant by 9/30/1999. Six months have now passed (7/31/1997), and the chipmunks have ridden their ponies into the vegetable garden. Earlier I included four examples of this migration (reintroduction of noncompliant CalcMaster), including a small merger and Frank Edwards' nifty, automatic expense-report generator. Now let's examine what a Risk Management Analysis run on 7/31/1997 says about our efforts to make CalcMaster compliant.

RISK MANAGEMENT PHASE ONE:
SUMMARY

The Risk Management Analysis, like the preceding analyses, starts with a summary. This first phase begins by presenting the Year 2000 countdown. The summary then outlines the current state of affairs.

SUMMARY

As of July 31, 1997, there are 884 days until January 1, 2000.

This analysis assumes all product releases of CalcMaster prior to version 3.0 are At-Risk. Only desktops running the MS-Windows operating system are included in this analysis.

There are 7,285 desktops with 7,415 installed copies of CalcMaster. Of these, 3,901 desktops (53.5%) are At-Risk. The largest number of At-Risk desktops is 1,350 in Admin. Based on the current rate of progress, all At-Risk desktop exposures will be eliminated by October 2000.

How many desktops are currently in the enterprise? The summary table reveals that we have picked up an additional 200 desktops (7,285-7,085) since running the January Risk Correction Analysis (see page 46). How many copies of CalcMaster are installed? We now have 281 more copies of CalcMaster (7,415-7,134) installed than were discovered in our January Risk Assessment Analysis (see page 31). The summary then goes on to tell us what percentage of these are noncompliant, and finishes with a punch to the gut. We are going to be compliant when? October 2000!

It would seem that the chipmunks have been busy, and our plan to make CalcMaster fully compliant by 9/30/1999 may not be on track. The summary projects a compliance date of October 2000. This projection shows us thirteen months behind plan (October 2000 - September 1999), with a ten-month noncompliance exposure (January 2000 through October 2000). Depending on the nature of the application, and how pervasive the application is within the enterprise, this ten-month risk window may or may not be acceptable. In this case, having a popular spreadsheet out of compliance is not an acceptable risk.

Before moving on to the next phase of the Risk Management Analysis, I should note I do not recommend that you wait six months before running this analysis. I believe that each compliance effort (application) should be monitored monthly. By running the analysis monthly, flaws in your compliance plan can be corrected, and you can react to evolutionary movement in the enterprise. Distributing copies of these monthly analyses to the appropriate corporate and department management is an effective means of keeping the compliance issue visible, and (if required) enlisting additional support.

RISK MANAGEMENT PHASE TWO: RISK DISTRIBUTION BY RISK LEVEL

Having just discovered in the summary that we are falling behind in our efforts to make CalcMaster compliant, we need to better understand our current risk base. Phase two of the Risk Management Analysis presents this corporate risk distribution in pie chart format.

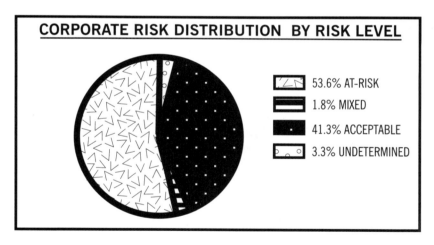

CORPORATE RISK DISTRIBUTION BY RISK LEVEL

53.6% AT-RISK
1.8% MIXED
41.3% ACCEPTABLE
3.3% UNDETERMINED

Understanding the distribution of risk levels becomes increasingly important as you execute your compliance program. Ignoring risk level distribution can mask both success and failure. For example, if a large percentage of your desktops fell in the Mixed category (both a compliant and noncompliant version installed), you may have a compatibility issue with the compliant version of the product. That is, if users can't run their older spreadsheets on the new version, they would hold onto the non-compliant version. Therefore, some compatibility initiative must be undertaken or your end users will willingly carry noncompliant code into the next century.

Equally deserving of investigation would be a large percentage of Undetermined desktops. Here the news might be good or bad because you may either be installing a compliant version of CalcMaster that is not recognized as such or a noncompliant version is "hiding." These situations are more common than you may suspect because special versions of an application frequently seep their way into the enterprise. An example of this might be a department of 200 users that experienced problems with version 2.9 of CalcMaster (noncompliant) when it was first installed. In an effort to address the problem, the supplier of the application made a beta version of CalcMaster version 3.0 (compliant) available for the affected desktops. This version of the product, labeled "Beta-12-3-96," would not have a recognizable version number and thus would be reported as Undetermined.

It is not important to understand all of the reasons that an application may be reported as Undetermined. What is important is that you have a program in place to investigate any significant number of undetermined copies that become part of a correction effort.

The final two slices of the pie (At-Risk and Acceptable), when taken together, present a high-level status of the problem. It would only take a quick look at the previous example to see that you have more At-Risk CalcMaster desktops than you have Acceptable CalcMaster desktops. Together, these two slices present a snapshot of CalcMaster compliance because—without comment, reflection, or projection—they tell you of your risk as of this moment in time. This "gut check" is especially useful as you sort through dozens of compliance issues, looking for those that deserve your attention.

Once we understand what the risk is, we need to understand where it resides. The next phase of the Risk Management Analysis distributes the current risk across the various business units.

CURRENT CORPORATE DISTRIBUTION OF RISK LEVELS BY DEPARTMENT					
DEPT.	AT-RISK	ACCEPTABLE	MIXED	UNDETERM.	**TOTAL**
SALES	200	1,321	101	129	**1,751**
R&D	1,050	800	12	47	**1,909**
FINANCE	843	140	3	13	**999**
ADMIN	1,350	422	6	23	**1,801**
OTHER	458	327	8	32	**825**
TOTAL	**3,901**	**3,010**	**130**	**244**	**7,285**

Having this table as part of the analysis is especially important because many compliance efforts include prioritizing the impact on users. In the case of CalcMaster, compliance was deemed acute for finance and sales. This table allows you to identify your current compliance risk by business function.

RISK MANAGEMENT PHASE FOUR:
TREND ANALYSIS

The next phase of the Risk Management Analysis is reminiscent of the last time we were ill and visited the doctor. The first question during such a visit, "Tell me how you feel," is addressed by the first three phases of the Risk Management Analysis. The fourth phase answers the doctor's next two questions, "When did you start feeling this way?" and "Are you getting better or worse?" In this case, the CalcMaster patient is not doing too well.

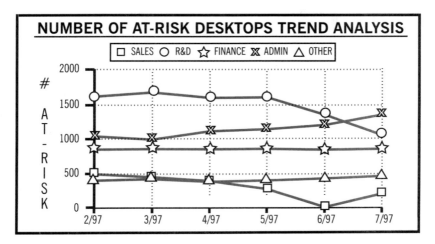

NUMBER OF AT-RISK DESKTOPS TREND ANALYSIS

□ SALES ○ R&D ☆ FINANCE ✕ ADMIN △ OTHER

This phase of the analysis plots a six-month trend for each business unit. It is this chart that maps most closely to the compliance plan for the application. Most compliance efforts are implemented over an extended period, with milestones being tied to various moments in time. For example, we may have scheduled a contractor to begin a ninety-day CalcMaster compliance effort for finance on 5/1/1997. This chart would be invaluable in tracking the progress of that effort. To more completely understand the value of this chart, we need to examine some of the trend lines in the example.

The first trend line that deserves consideration is finance. This is a department that we identified as critical, but it has experienced no progress in eliminating the CalcMaster compliance problem. Of course, this could be the result of the correction schedule, contractor availability, or some internal factor unique to the finance department (e.g., not wanting to disturb the desktops during year-end closing). Generally speaking, however, this flat line should be a cause for alarm in that there are only so many six-month windows between now and 12/31/1999. In addition, there are reasons that this line, exclusive of the correction effort (e.g., desktop replacement), should naturally trend downward.

Looking at the R&D curve, we see some positive news...perhaps. No doubt, fewer at-risk desktops within a department, by any measure, is a positive development. What if, however, that department was scheduled to be fully compliant by the end of June 1997? In that case, the news would lose some of its luster. Another question comes to mind: why is R&D showing more progress than finance? It could be a matter of budget considerations, they could have a higher rate of desktop replacement, or it could be a contractor improvising. Regardless, comparison of the two curves allows us to consider the issue.

The administration curve is most disturbing. Here is a department that has the largest number of noncompliant copies of CalcMaster, and they are adding more! This could be the result of a merger. More likely, they added or replaced desktops, but failed to modify the standard configuration they order from their supplier. In any case, this trend deserves immediate attention. As Bob Helms, my CIO put it, "I'm having enough trouble wrestling the beast. I don't need to be feeding it!"

The sales curve also presents a unique picture. The message here is clear—just because you killed it doesn't mean it's dead. As we will see in the upcoming case study (chapter 9), there is a phoenix-like quality to Year 2000 compliance problems. In the case of sales, we discover the ashes of victory, and from those ashes arises a new phoenix of noncompliance. Specifically, the curve shows the eradication of noncompliant CalcMaster (within sales) in June, and 200 new CalcMaster compliance problems in July. As we have already highlighted a number of reasons noncompliant code can resurface, I will not speculate on the possible reasons for 200 new errant copies.

Maintaining the gains we make in enterprise compliance can be frustrating and expensive, as errant code can populate much faster than it can be corrected. The trick to preventing setbacks in a compliance effort is using a technique known as "compliance auditing." Compliance auditing requires an electronic auditing feature in the asset tracking system (see chapter 2) that you selected. This auditing component automatically notifies you when a specific standard within the enterprise is violated (e.g., when a new copy of a noncompliant application appears in the enterprise). Such a feature would have electronically notified us (via system alerts or e-mail) as soon as a noncompliant copy of CalcMaster appeared on a sales desktop, allowing us to stem the flow of additional noncompliant copies.

RISK MANAGEMENT PHASE FIVE:
RISK COUNTDOWN

The next phase of the Risk Management Analysis brings to mind a professional basketball game I was watching earlier this year. It was the deciding game of a play-off series. The announcers were waxing on about complex game strategies and the intricacies of how the opposing players matched up against one another. Into this picture stepped the acknowledged star of the game. The announcers were quick to engage him in a discussion of their theories. As the camera cut to a full face shot of the star, an off-camera announcer asked, "What do you see as the key to winning the series today?" The star blinked once and with the cold precision of a surgeon replied, "When the game is over, we need to have scored the most points."

In this focused response, we are reminded of the simple nature of our own mission. All of this—the budgets, interdependent applications, scarce resources, an evolving enterprise, and more—ultimately rests on a single point. It is this point, 12/31/1999, that is the focus of the fifth phase. It forces us to face the camera and answer the question, "Where are we going to be when time runs out?"

The Risk Countdown projects our past efforts into the future. The chart presents three sets of data points across a time scale that begins with the initiation of the project and concludes with a projected date of compliance. The first set of data points is represented by the solid line to the left of the vertical line labeled Current. It tracks the actual number (the Historical Rate) of noncompliant versions of CalcMaster from the inception of the project to the date of the analysis. The dotted line (to the right of the vertical Current line—the Projected Rate) extrapolates this trend into the future, arriving at a projected compliance date. The final series (represented by a line with dashes—the Required Rate) tracks a trend that leads to full compliance by 12/31/1999.

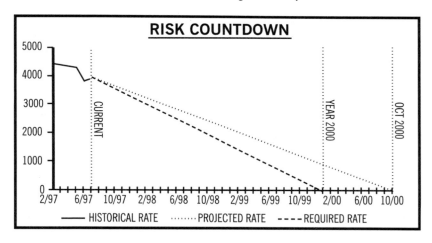

The area between the Projected Rate and the Required Rate defines the noncompliance risk for CalcMaster. This is the projected amount of time that CalcMaster will not be compliant. Some mid-level managers viewing this phase of the analysis for the first time often see "flaws" in its methodology. In reality, it is their perspective and not the analysis that needs to be corrected. The two points of contention have to do with the targeted objective and the number of affected desktops.

The first of these alleged flaws (targeted objective) cites the fact that the projected curve, although not compliant, may indeed be the agreed-to compliance plan. The argument then becomes that the compliance line (Year 2000) should be moved out to the desired project plan date. This makes the invalid assumption that the objective of this phase is some form of project management. It is not. Its intent is to give executives a quantifiable understanding of the Year 2000 risk for that specific application. It makes little difference if the risk is planned, or the result of incompetence; the consequence of the exposure is constant. It is the potential for facing those consequences that interests senior management.

The second dubious correction that some would make to this phase involves the number of desktops affected. In this case, a threshold of tolerance is proposed, allowing for a "reasonably" small percentage of noncompliant copies to be present in the enterprise and still be charted as compliant. A CIO friend of mine once described this type of reasoning as "nothing more than a negative lottery, in that your chances of suffering disaster might be small, but if it happens, no one gives a damn about the odds." All levels of management need full disclosure of the risks associated with the Year 2000. Try to avoid any suggestions that attempt to perfume the pig.

RISK MANAGEMENT PHASE SIX: CORRECTIONS PER MONTH TO MEET DEADLINE

The final phase of the Risk Management Analysis (phase six—see following page) translates the compliance effort into a different currency. It presents the number of desktops that need to be corrected each month (by department) if CalcMaster is to be compliant by December 31, 1999. This translation is helpful in developing a corollary between time, available resources, and volume. For example, with your knowledge of the various departments, their corresponding budgets, technical expertise, and IT support staff, the idea of finance being able to correct at least twenty-nine desktops every month from now until the Year 2000 might be laughable. This may not be as obvious when considered as 843 corrections by 12/31/1999.

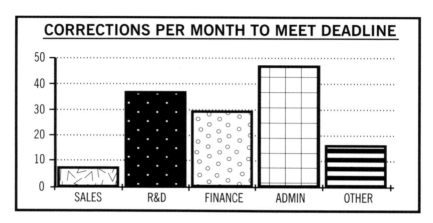

The other advantage of this clocked countdown is its digestibility. When you are counting on others to assist you (contractors, departmental/division personnel, end users, etc.) in meeting compliance, translating the task to a protracted sustained effort can be helpful. Telling R&D in July that they have to deal with 1,050 problems over the next two and one-half years might encourage procrastination. Showing them that compliance equates to correcting at least thirty-six desktops each and every month until the Year 2000 presents a more compelling reason for action.

This final phase of the analysis may be helpful in minimizing "contractor compression." Year 2000 contractors are resource constrained. They are unable to hire the staff necessary to fulfill current contracts, yet they continue to take on additional opportunities. It is for this reason that many organizations will find the compliance schedules slipping (deliverables compressed toward the end of the contract) as resources fall short, or are siphoned off to other contracts. Those firms that can present a clear and consistent performance measure to their contractors (during regular status meetings) will have a distinct advantage over those that merely express alarm. Consistently presenting your contractor with an ever-mounting number of corrections that must be accomplished each month highlights the compression of the effort to both the contractor and project manager. Better yet, why not use corrections per month as one of the measures of contract compliance?

Again, the value of the analysis can best be appreciated by looking at all of the phases on a single page.

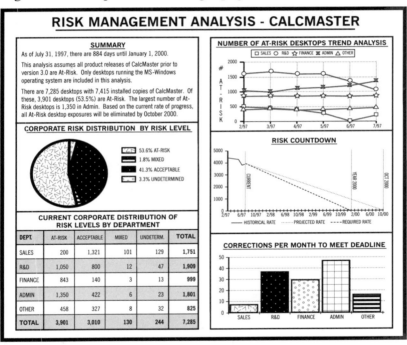

A final word of caution about contractor management. I believe that most Year 2000 contractors are interested in fully meeting the terms of their obligations. They are not knowingly contracting for business that they do not have resources to fulfill. They are, however, overestimating the productivity of their existing resources, and are driving their business on the assumption of an aggressive hiring plan of resources that are increasingly scarce.

It is for this reason that many contractors will find themselves unable to meet the terms of their Year 2000 compliance contracts. Interestingly, many organizations are relying on their standard contract mechanisms to manage their Year 2000 contractors. Typically the big stick in this arsenal is having some progress payment withheld and/or terminating the contract. Now consider the following scenario. You have a two-and-one-half-year agreement with a contractor for Year 2000 enterprise compliance. After one year of watching the effort become alarmingly compressed, you invoke your right to terminate the agreement. Have you just punished your contractor or done him a favor?

In this situation we find the Year 2000 twelve months closer, and available resources are more scarce (see page 50 for the Chris Jesse 15 percent rule). In reality, you may have done your former contractor a favor by allowing him to replace your business with a more lucrative contract. Further, the new contractor you hire will cost you more and will be less willing to accept severe penalties for contract violations. Clearly, the old rules of contractor management suffer when translated to the Year 2000 economy. Penalties and terminations are not a currency that converts favorably in the compressed world of Year 2000 compliance.

It is for this reason that we must increasingly rely on the integrity of our contractor partners and give those partners the measurements necessary to meet their obligations. Here is perhaps the most compelling reason for having an asset tracking system with a Year 2000 compliance module. Without it, how will you know what to contract for, how will you monitor the progress of the effort, and how will you certify that the Year 2000 risk has been eliminated?

By running the Risk Management Analysis each month, you will have the tools to proactively manage both the compliance risk and those charged with implementing the compliance initiatives. In addition, these analyses, distributed to the senior management team, will allow the Year 2000 czar to keep the executive team involved in the compliance effort.

Year 2000 enterprise compliance is a moving target. Even the best of managers will find themselves frustrated by the fluid and sometimes nebulous nature of such an effort. It is only through the disciplined, periodic use of tools, such as the Risk Management Analysis, that a platform of knowledge can be sustained. And it is from this base of information that we are able to estimate risks, manage resources, justify increased funding, and maintain the support of all levels of management.

SUMMARY

When my friends caught me with a bucket accidentally stuck on my head, I told them that I planned the whole thing. What else was I supposed to do? I didn't want to look stupid!

CHAPTER 9

ONCE UPON A TIME
CASE STUDY

Me: Happy Birthday! *(Delivering a giant, white, twelve-year-old Ford)*

Rachel (my daughter): *(Obviously miffed)* Thanks a lot.

Me: What's wrong?

Rachel: I wanted a Honda Prelude.

Me: I want to be an astronaut.

Rachel: *(Irritated)* No kidding, I really wanted a little sports car.

Me: I really understand because I really want to be an astronaut.

Rachel: *(Frustrated)* Just forget it.

By the time Rachel was twenty, she had learned to love that old Ford. It gave her five years of worthy service, and I think she would tell you that she felt a pang in her heart when she sent "Elvira" off to the junk yard. This story, though, is not about Rachel's car, but rather her fairy tale. Rachel at sixteen had developed the skill of fashioning a false reality around her desires. Within her reality, she saw herself driving down the road in a hot little sports car. Unfortunately for her, the person funding the acquisition saw this new driver surrounded with as much mass as possible. It would be just a matter of weeks before our perceptions of reality would merge.

My new driver had gone shopping on a Saturday afternoon, and had her mind on something other than her driving as she left the mall parking lot. Rachel thought she had looked left before crossing traffic, but in a split second discovered that she had made a mistake. A car going forty miles per hour slammed on its brakes, but it was too late. The car crashed into the left (driver's) side of the Ford doing several thousand dollars of damage. Fortunately, neither Rachel nor the other driver suffered physical injury. Her pride was not so lucky, however, for it was in desperate need of first aid. As I arrived on the scene of the accident, she approached me with a short but sincere confession: "The accident was my fault, and I am glad I was in a big car."

I bring you this story to deliver two messages. First, having seen three children through their first five years of driving, I give you the following irrefutable equation: New Drivers = Big Slow Cars. And second, if you think you can successfully manage enterprise Year 2000 compliance without a proactive asset tracking system, then I have but one thing to say: "I want to be an astronaut."

Believing that enterprise compliance can be attained via a massive technology refresh (replacement of all enterprise desktops) or through the establishment of standards is a fairy tale. For with all the pressure to locate funds for the Year 2000 compliance effort, it is unlikely that there will be money to entertain a massive refresh of all enterprise desktops prior to 12/31/1999. The idea of standards is an equally fanciful solution because standards must be implemented, monitored, and enforced to be an effective compliance vehicle. How are you going to accomplish this implementation, monitoring, and enforcement without proactive asset tracking?

Even a combined total refresh of the enterprise desktop population, along with a strong standards effort, would not accomplish compliance. Users and departments will always seek a means of achieving their primary mission, even if unknowingly wreaking havoc on your compliance initiative. And if we are honest, we must admit that the users and departments are correct. For the mission of every business is some form of product or service, not compliance. It would be a fairy tale, indeed, for us to believe that the business enterprise would subordinate itself to a compliance initiative.

During speaking engagements, I occasionally run across those who continue to construct their own compliance reality. They cling to the notion that old practices, such as annual physical inventories and standards, can lead them to enterprise Year 2000 compliance. For these folks, I construct an idyllic compliance fairy tale. The story allows them to indulge their own reality, but at the same time highlights the fact that they are about to pull into traffic and be hit broadside. Here then, for those who see a solution in past methods, is the best that can be hoped for...

A COMPLIANCE FAIRY TALE...

Once upon a time, there was an executive charged with making the enterprise Year 2000 compliant. Because he had led a good life and eaten all his broccoli, he had only one application that was noncompliant. Not only that, he knew which application was in error, and that it was isolated to a specific job function. "Stop!" you say, "This isn't realistic. Enterprises have dozens of problems spread across scores of job functions." You are, of course, correct, but this is my fairy tale so mind your own business.

Where was I? Oh yes, a single application isolated to a specific function... Our hero faced the task of ridding Global Bank's enterprise (60,000 desktops) of the errant application (BondSwap) that the bank's investment traders used to optimize returns on bond trades. Our hero, being steeped in knowledge of the bank, immediately recognized that bonds are very date sensitive and that erroneous bond trades could have a significant cents-per-share impact if not corrected.

It is with this revelation that our handsome young executive…"Stop!" you say, "Anyone who works with compliance issues across a distributed enterprise is old and grizzled about twenty minutes after taking the job." Look, if you keep interrupting, I am going to start over. It's a feel-good fairy tale. OK? If I want to make him young and handsome, he is young and handsome!

As I was saying before being so rudely interrupted… And so our young, handsome, extremely rich executive with the beautiful wife and a golf handicap of two, set about the task of finding the employees who were using the BondSwap application. Just then the phone rang. It was the senior vice president of personnel, and she had heard of our hero's problem. "Let me help," she begged. "I will produce a list of all employees who have bond trading in their title or job description, and cross-reference it to their office mailing address. Would you like their phone number as well?" Our hero graciously accepted, asking if he could have the list before lunch.

"Stop! Stop! Stop! Stop! Stop it!" you say. "No one ever volunteers to help like this, and if they do, you are lucky to see it before your next birthday!" Look, I have already warned you about interrupting once. You want something to get excited about? Here take this…

"Of course you can have them by lunch," the personnel VP replied. "In fact, why don't I prepare a set of mailing labels for you as well." Get the message? One more word out of you and I am going to make this guy an Olympic gold medal winner too.

After a tasty lunch at the club, our hero returned to work to find the list and labels prepared. In addition, his compliance manager had anticipated his strategy and prepared 983 diskettes with the compliant version of the BondSwap application. He quickly looked at the label count (983) and thought this must be his lucky day, just the right number of diskettes for the number of non-compliant users. Just then, his assistant entered with 983 letters individually addressed to each user. The letter explained the problem and provided installation instructions.

His assistant could see that the strain of this whole effort was beginning to show on our hero, so she made him an offer he couldn't refuse. "Why don't you let me sign these letters and overnight them with a diskette to each of the users. In the meantime, I have arranged for a 2:30 tee time at the club. You have worked really hard; you deserve a break."

And so it was that our hero sent a compliant copy of the BondSwap application to each of the bond traders. They, recognizing his name on the attached letter, immediately dropped everything they were doing and installed the compliant version of the software on their respective desktops. Look, it could happen... end users cooperating in locked step...it could happen. It may take a combination of drugs, lottery-like luck, and a visit from a punch-drunk enforcer, but 983 end users could cooperate.

In a moment of triumph, our hero arrived at work at 11:00 the next morning to a fully compliant enterprise. All that was left to do was call Tiger and give him a chance to win back the money he lost in yesterday's golf match, and give his boss the thumbs up.

And they all almost lived happily ever after.

The End.

I'm sorry, what did you say? What do I mean by almost happily ever after? Well, there is a minor correction that would have to be made to the story if you are looking for an unqualified "happily ever after." If we just correct one thing, I think we are there.

It seems that some of the users, when installing the new version of the compliant software, forgot to delete the old. Some future user of the system mistakenly clicked on the old application and issued some bad trades. We can fix the story by simply having the old application deleted as part of the installation process for the compliant application. There now, all better.

And they all lived kind of happily ever after.

The End.

I'm sorry, I forgot about the other thing. About fifty of the users had trouble with their disk drives and had to go to a back-up tape. In the process they restored the noncompliant version of BondSwap. No problem, we will just change the story so that all back-up tapes were altered so that they contained only compliant versions of BondSwap. Don't look at me that way... I don't know how we do it; it's a fairy tale, give me a break!

And so, they all lived or survived happily ever after.

The End.

I know, I know, it feels like we are moving backward, but there was another big problem with BondSwap. I think we need to correct it too if you want the whole (happily ever after) enchilada. It seems that some of the traders had (over time) taken a copy of the noncompliant version of BondSwap home and installed it on their home computer. This allowed them to dial in in the middle of the night and conduct transactions in the Far East. We will just change the story so that they fix their work and home copies of BondSwap. Finally...

And so they sought protection from the courts, suffered a Securities and Exchange Commission investigation, and began responding to shareholder lawsuits.

The End.

Oops, I didn't know about those copies. It seems that bond traders are as overworked as the rest of us and delegate some of their routine work (trades) to various assistants. Over the years, they had installed noncompliant copies of BondSwap on individuals' machines whose job title had no recorded relationship to bond trading.

As it turns out, there were really 1,370 copies of BondSwap installed. The 983 reported by the personnel department as bond traders, and 387 copies distributed to others so they might handle the more routine transactions. It is from these noncompliant desktops that ninety date-impaired trades were made during the first workday of the Year 2000. Hmmm, I guess we are going to have to amend the story so that we somehow supernaturally know all the desktops in the enterprise that have the BondSwap application. Now all we need to do is rewrite the story so that all 1,370 end users get the fix and correctly install it and...

They all lived happily ever after...except for those who did not have the proper configuration to support the new version.

The End.

No problem, no problem, just give me a minute. I just need to give our hero total knowledge of the enterprise and how it is evolving, and have him deliver the necessary equipment and software upgrades to the proper desktops along with the letter and corrected application, and there!

And so they lived in chaos and hostility ever after. No, wait, I can fix this too. He had all the funding he needed and had the resources necessary to implement the required changes at all the required locations at the proper time.

And so they all lived happily ever after.

The End.

I guess those who touted traditional methodologies are right. You really don't need an asset tracking solution to address your enterprise Year 2000 compliance effort. All that is required is an active imagination, a flexible view of reality, and a few rewrites. Of course, we were only dealing with one easily identified application, within one job function, where the problem only involved a small percentage of the enterprise.

Perhaps I should write another fairy tale that incorporates all of those elements? On second thought, it might just be easier on each of us for you to install an effective asset tracking system with a Year 2000 compliance module.

P.S. Our hero had lifts in his shoes, cheated at golf, lied about his age, wore a fake Rolex watch, and Tiger (Swartz) won his money back and then some. Oh well, I understand. I wanted to be an astronaut.

SUMMARY

Our desires entertain us in hushed whispers. For they fear awakening the attention of two uninvited companions—our logic and our experience.

CHAPTER 10

• SAVE THE BOX •

Mary (my married daughter): I just called to tell you that Rob and I finally bought a lawn mower.

Me: Did you take my advice and get a four-stroke engine, light mower deck, and a grass catcher?

Mary: No, we got a push mower.

Me: As in no engine, struggle with each blade of grass? Get Rob on the phone. *(Rob, on the extension, joins the conversation.)*

Me: Listen carefully to old Dad. Save the receipt and box, it's going back.

Mary and Rob: You don't understand, we're looking forward to the exercise.

Me: Save the box.

Mary and Rob: We feel good about not polluting the environ…

Me: Save the box.

Mary and Rob: You know this mower will save a lot on gas and maintenance.

Me: Save the box.

Rob: *(Two hours later)* Just called to tell you that outside of the rocks jamming this thing every three feet, the hills, and the fact that I could chew the grass faster than this thing can mow, it's really going well. There is a bright side, however…

Me: What's that?

Rob: We did save the box.

Mary and Rob returned the push mower and got a great deal on a four-cycle mower, with a light deck and a grass catcher. In the process, they learned that sometimes age (experience) brings a more acute vision of both opportunity and folly.

The lesson in this, however, is not about their ignoring my plea for sanity, but about their subordinating the obvious to the trivial. For if they were really interested in saving the environment, they should more wisely plan their trips to the store. Just avoiding three trips a year would more than offset thirty weeks of lawn mowing. As for the exercise, use the time you save with a power mower to occasionally walk to the store! I think we have a double hitter here—exercise and ecology. Finally, does anyone remember how many times each year you had to get the blades on a manual mower sharpened?

Somewhere amid all the clutter of good intentions, Mary and Rob forgot that their objective was to mow their half-acre lot. It was this objective that should have been their focus. All else should have been considered a secondary, if not an incidental benefit. Mary and Rob discovered what wise men have known for ages. The grandest of all castles are built on basic foundations.

Within Mary and Rob's lesson, we can see the truth about Year 2000 compliance efforts for the enterprise. This undertaking is not the mission, but rather an auxiliary benefit. In reality, the mission is having control of your distributed enterprise (i.e., understanding what you have, how it is changing over time, and where all of this is occurring).

As for all of the specialized Year 2000 compliance tools discussed in this text, they are actually free. For unlike other Year 2000 expenditures whose utility expires with the completion of the compliance effort, the tools discussed in this text continue to provide invaluable benefits long after the Year 2000 hoopla has been forgotten. These same tools, which assess risk, compute correction costs, and manage risk, are equally valuable in the planning and implementation of any change to the distributed enterprise. Consider for a moment the complexity of upgrading all the desktops within the enterprise to the latest version of an operating system. The same planning is needed, and the same principles apply. It is only the mission that changes.

So where do you go from here? I cannot begin to give you a detailed plan that addresses the specifics of your compliance effort. Each executive responsible for compliance must build a plan around available resources and the unique features of both their business and computing enterprise. There are, however, seven common steps that I believe are essential to any successful enterprise compliance plan:

1) *Implement an effective asset tracking solution.* I describe the benefits and features of such a solution in *A Journey Through Oz.* Buy or borrow a copy. Personally, I prefer the buy option (contact the publisher) as I am putting two children through college. In addition, there is an evaluation checklist available for asset tracking solutions. If you have an interest in this document, drop me an e-mail at chrisj@tangram.com or request it from the asset tracking Web site (www.assettracking.com), and I will see to it that you are sent a free copy.

2) *Follow an organized methodology* (e.g., risk identification, risk assessment, risk correction, compliance planning, compliance modeling, and risk management). Creating a unique means of addressing each compliance issue is expensive, confusing, and defies accountability. It is only in comparing our problem on a level playing field that we can mix and match an optimal solution.

3) *Continue the identification process.* Having an effective compliance program does not inoculate you against additional compliance issues. While implementing your asset tracking solution, you should continue the identification process outlined in chapter 3. New noncompliant applications will continue to surface until the last minute. Maintain an active identification effort.

4) *Do not distribute the various steps of your compliance effort to different individuals.* The same person/team should handle all steps of the compliance effort. In other words, once CalcMaster is identified as a problem, the same team should see it through all six steps of the compliance process. There are already too many variables and complexities associated with a distributed enterprise compliance effort. There is no need to add lack of accountability to the equation.

5) *Build time into your schedule for iterative efforts.* As we discussed in chapter 8, applications on desktops have a way of slipping back to the dark side (reverting to noncompliance). In addition, further delays can be expected if you are not using a Compliance Modeling tool (see mismatched corrections in chapter 7). Without knowing the tools, funding, and specifics of the enterprise, it is difficult to suggest a specific cushion to build into your time estimates. It is safe to say, however, that anything less than a 20 percent cushion is looking for trouble, and anything more than 40 percent is an indication that you have inadequate staff (or contractors) or have selected the wrong tools.

6) *Publish, publish, and publish some more.* Make the compliance analyses available as broadly as possible. In widely distributing these analyses to both senior and departmental executives, you demonstrate a coordinated effort, present the scope of the problem, and most important, make them feel like they are part of the initiative. This point will prove

to be especially valuable should you find it necessary to seek additional funding.

7) *Hold monthly status reviews.* Force those responsible to present the status of each noncompliant application. Structuring these sessions around the analyses described in this book provides a consistent means of presentation that will ensure that all key elements of the compliance effort are addressed. Such reviews should include both employee and contractor personnel.

That is all there is to it (except for the twelve-hour days and sleepless nights). So relax, have a good time, and stay loose. They will try to blame the turn of the century on you, but it won't stick. They will accuse you of not fixing their problems, but you can prove otherwise. And besides, if you were looking for friends and glory, you never would have taken the assignment in the first place.

The zoo is waiting, the animals are hungry, and it is time to teach the chipmunks to dance. Thanks for reading the book. If you have any comments, or need help locating chipmunk-sized tutus, feel free to drop me an e-mail at chrisj@tangram.com. If you would like to receive copies of other Year 2000 material that I have written, turn the page for more information. Now on with the show!

SUMMARY

What we label as the "basics" are not basic at all—they are the essentials, for nothing moves forward until they are served.

ADDITIONAL INFORMATION

Other material I have written on this topic includes, "The Quantification of Year 2000 Risks for the Distributed Enterprise," and "An Evaluation Checklist for Distributed Year 2000 Solutions." The first document (Quantification of Risks) uses a grid methodology to help quantify the impact that a specific compliance issue will have on an organization. The second document (Evaluation Checklist) is a table-based scoring system that helps identify both the mandatory and desirable features of a Year 2000 compliance solution. Unfortunately, neither of these documents fit the format of this book. I do, however, make them available free of charge to the reader. If you have an interest in receiving a copy of one or both of these documents, simply drop me an e-mail (chrisj@tangram.com) and include the ISBN number on the back cover of the book. Depending on my assistant's schedule, such requests are generally turned around in two to ten days.

INDEX

B

C

D

I

J

L

M

O

P

R